KT-418-256

PRAYERS THAT AVAIL MUCH®

For Men

PRAYERS THAT AVAIL MUCH®

For Men

by
Germaine Copeland

Harrison House
Tulsa, Oklahoma

06 05 04 03 02   8 7 6 5 4

Prayers That Avail Much° for Men
ISBN 157794-182-9
Copyright © 1999 by Germaine Copeland
38 Sloan Street
Roswell, Georgia 30075

Published by Harrison House, Inc.
P.O. Box 35035
Tulsa, Oklahoma 74153

CONTENTS

Part IV: Prayers for Ministry

How to Pray Prayers That Avail Much®

The prayers in this book are to be used by you for yourself and for others. They are a matter of the heart. Deliberately pray and meditate on each prayer. Allow the Holy Spirit to make the Word a reality in your heart. Your spirit will become alive to God's Word, and you will begin to think like God thinks and talk like He talks. You will find yourself pouring over His Word— hungering for more and more. The Father rewards those who diligently seek Him (Heb. 11:6).

Research and contemplate the spiritual significance of each verse listed with the prayers. These are by no means the only Scriptures on certain subjects, but they are a beginning.

These prayers are a guide for you to have a more intimate relationship with your heavenly Father. The study of His Word transforms your mind and lifestyle. Then, others will know that it is possible to change, and you will give hope to those who come to you seeking advice. When you admonish someone with the Word, you are offering spiritual guidance and consolation.

Walk in God's counsel, and prize His wisdom (Ps. 1; Prov. 4:7,8). People are looking for something on which they can depend. When someone in need comes to you, you can point him to that portion in God's Word that is the answer to his problem. You become victorious, trustworthy and the one with the answer, for your heart is fixed and established on His Word (Ps. 112).

Once you begin delving into God's Word, you must commit to ordering your conversation aright (Ps. 50:23). That is being a doer of the Word. Faith always has a good report. You cannot pray effectively for yourself, for someone else or about something and then talk negatively about the matter (Matt. 12:34-37). This is being double-minded, and a double-minded man receives *nothing* from God (James 1:6-8).

In Ephesians 4:29-30 AMP it is written:

> Let no foul or polluting language, nor evil word, nor unwholesome or worthless talk [ever] come out of your mouth; but only such [speech] as is good and beneficial to the spiritual progress of others, as is fitting to the need

and the occasion, that it may be a blessing and give grace (God's favor) to those who hear it.

And do not grieve the Holy Spirit of God, (do not offend, or vex, or sadden Him) by whom you were sealed (marked, branded as God's own, secured) for the day of redemption—of final deliverance through Christ from evil and the consequences of sin.

Reflect on these words and give them time to keep your perspective in line with God's will. Our Father has much, so very much, to say about that little member, the tongue (James 3). Give the devil no opportunity by getting into worry, unforgiveness, strife and criticism. Put a stop to idle and foolish talking (Eph. 4:27; 5:4). You are to be a blessing to others (Gal. 6:10).

Talk the answer, not the problem. The answer is in God's Word. You must have knowledge of that Word— revelation knowledge (1 Cor. 2:7-16). The Holy Spirit, your teacher, will reveal the things that have been freely given to us by God (John 14:26).

As an intercessor, unite with others in prayer. United prayer is a mighty weapon that the Body of Christ is to use.

Have the faith of God, and approach Him confidently. When you pray according to His will, He hears you. Then you know you have what you ask of Him (1 John 5:14-15 NIV). Do not throw away your confidence. It will be richly rewarded (Hebrews 10:35 NIV). Allow your spirit to pray by the Holy Spirit. Praise God for the victory now before any manifestation. *Walk by faith and not by sight* (2 Cor. 5:7).

When your faith comes under pressure, don't be moved. As Satan attempts to challenge you, resist him steadfast in the faith—letting patience have her perfect work (James 1:4). Take the Sword of the Spirit and the shield of faith and quench his every fiery dart (Eph. 6:16,17). The entire substitutionary work of Christ was for you. Satan is now a defeated foe because Jesus conquered him (Col. 2:14,15). Satan is overcome by the blood of the Lamb and the Word of our testimony (Rev. 12:11). Fight the good fight of faith (1 Tim. 6:12). Withstand the adversary and be firm in faith against his onset—rooted, established, strong and determined (1 Pet. 5:9). Speak God's Word boldly and courageously.

Your desire should be to please and to bless the Father. As you pray according to His Word, He joyfully hears that you—His child—are living and walking in the truth (3 John 4).

How exciting to know that the prayers of the saints are forever in the throne room (Rev. 5:8). Hallelujah!

Praise God for His Word and the limitlessness of prayer in the name of Jesus. It belongs to every child of God. Therefore, run with patience the race that is set before you, looking unto Jesus the Author and Finisher of your faith (Heb. 12:1,2). God's Word is able to build you up and give you your rightful inheritance among all God's set apart ones (Acts 20:32).

Commit yourself to pray and to pray correctly by approaching the throne with your mouth filled with His Word!

Personal Confessions

Jesus is Lord over my spirit, my soul and my body (Phil. 2:9-11).

Jesus has been made unto me wisdom, righteousness, sanctification and redemption. I can do all things through Christ Who strengthens me (1 Cor. 1:30; Phil. 4:13).

The Lord is my Shepherd. I do not want. My God supplies all my need according to His riches in glory in Christ Jesus (Ps. 23; Phil. 4:19).

I do not fret or have anxiety about anything. I do not have a care (Phil. 4:6; 1 Pet. 5:6,7).

I am the Body of Christ. I am redeemed from the curse, because Jesus bore my sicknesses and carried my diseases in His own body. By His stripes I am healed. I forbid any sickness or disease to operate in my body. Every organ, every tissue of my body functions in the perfection in which God created it to function. I honor God and bring glory to Him in my body (Gal. 3:13; Matt. 8:17; 1 Pet. 2:24; 1 Cor. 6:20).

I have the mind of Christ and hold the thoughts, feelings and purposes of His heart (1 Cor. 2:16).

I am a believer and not a doubter. I hold fast to my confession of faith. I decide to walk by faith and practice faith. My faith comes by hearing and hearing by the Word of God. Jesus is the Author and the Developer of my faith (Heb. 4:14; Heb. 11:6; Rom. 10:17; Heb. 12:2).

The love of God has been shed abroad in my heart by the Holy Spirit and His love abides in me richly. I keep myself in the Kingdom of light, in love, in the Word, and the wicked one touches me not (Rom. 5:5; 1 John 4:16; 1 John 5:18).

I tread upon serpents and scorpions and over all the power of the enemy. I take my shield of faith and quench his every fiery dart. Greater is He Who is in me than he who is in the world (Ps. 91:13; Eph. 6:16; 1 John 4:4).

I am delivered from this present evil world. I am seated with Christ in heavenly places. I reside in the Kingdom of God's dear Son. The law of the Spirit of

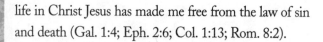

life in Christ Jesus has made me free from the law of sin
and death (Gal. 1:4; Eph. 2:6; Col. 1:13; Rom. 8:2).

I fear *not* for God has given me a spirit of power, of
love and of a sound mind. God is on my side (2 Tim.
1:7; Rom. 8:31).

I hear the voice of the Good Shepherd. I hear my
Father's voice, and the voice of a stranger I will not
follow. I roll my works upon the Lord. I commit and
trust them wholly to Him. He will cause my thoughts
to become agreeable to His will, and so shall my plans
be established and succeed (John 10:27; Prov. 16:3).

I am a world overcomer because I am born of God.
I represent the Father and Jesus well. I am a useful
member in the Body of Christ. I am His workmanship
re-created in Christ Jesus. My Father God is all the
while effectually at work in me both to will and do His
good pleasure (1 John 5:4-5; Eph. 2:10; Phil. 2:13).

I let the Word dwell in me richly. He Who began a
good work in me will continue until the day of Christ
(Col. 3:16; Phil. 1:6).

Part One

PRAYERS FOR PERSONAL NEEDS

To Receive Jesus as Savior and Lord

Father, it is written in Your Word that if I confess with my mouth that Jesus is Lord and believe in my heart that You have raised Him from the dead, I shall be saved. Therefore, Father, I confess that Jesus is my Lord. I make Him Lord of my life right now. I believe in my heart that You raised Jesus from the dead. I renounce my past life with Satan and close the door to any of his devices.

I thank You for forgiving me of all my sin. Jesus is my Lord, and I am a new creation. Old things have passed away. Now all things become new in Jesus' name. Amen.

Scripture References

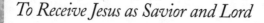

John 3:16	John 14:6
John 6:37	Romans 10:9,10
John 10:10b	Romans 10:13
Romans 3:23	Ephesians 2:1-10
2 Corinthians 5:19	2 Corinthians 5:17
John 16:8,9	John 1:12
Romans 5:8	2 Corinthians 5:21

Knowing God's Will

Father, I thank You that You are instructing me and teaching me in the way I should go and that You are guiding me with Your eye. I thank You for Your guidance and leadership concerning Your will, Your plan and Your purpose for my life. I do hear the voice of the Good Shepherd, for I know You and follow You. You lead me in the paths of righteousness for Your name's sake.

In the name of Jesus, I refuse to be conformed to this world (this age), [fashioned after and adapted to its external, superficial customs], but I submit to the transformation by the [entire] renewal of my mind [by its new ideals and its new attitude], so that I may prove [for myself] what is Your good and acceptable and perfect will, even the thing which is good and acceptable and perfect [in Your sight for me].

Thank You, Father, that my path is growing brighter and brighter until it reaches the full light of day. As I follow You, Lord, I believe my path is becoming clearer each day.

Thank You, Father, that Jesus was made unto me wisdom. Confusion is not a part of my life. I am not confused about Your will for me. I trust in You and lean not unto my own understanding. As I acknowledge You in all my ways, You direct my paths. I believe that as I trust in You completely, You will show me the path of life.

Thank You, Father, in Jesus' name. Amen.

Scripture References

Psalm 32:8	Proverbs 4:18
John 10:3,4	1 Corinthians 1:30
Psalm 23:3	Proverbs 3:5,6
Romans 12:2 AMP	Psalm 16:11

To Walk in the Word

Father, in the name of Jesus, *I commit myself to walk in the Word.* Your Word living in me produces Your life in this world. I recognize that Your Word is integrity itself—steadfast, sure, eternal—and I trust my life to its provisions.

You have sent Your Word forth into my heart. I let it dwell in me richly in all wisdom. I meditate in it day and night so that I may diligently act on it. The Incorruptible Seed, the Living Word, the Word of Truth, is abiding in my spirit. That Seed is growing mightily in me now, producing Your nature, Your life. It is my counsel, my shield, my buckler, my powerful weapon in battle. The Word is a lamp to my feet and a light to my path. It makes my way plain before me. I do not stumble, for my steps are ordered in the Word.

The Holy Spirit leads and guides me into all the truth. He gives me understanding, discernment and comprehension so that I am preserved from the snares of the evil one.

I delight myself in You and Your Word. Because of that, You put Your desires in my heart. I commit my way unto You, and You bring it to pass. I am confident that You are at work in me now both to will and to do all Your good pleasure.

I exalt Your Word, hold it in high esteem and give it first place. *I make my schedule around Your Word.* I make the Word final authority to settle all questions that confront me. I choose to agree with the Word of God, and I choose to disagree with any thoughts, conditions or circumstances contrary to Your Word. I boldly and confidently say that my heart is fixed and established on the solid foundation—the living Word of God! Amen.

Scripture References

Hebrews 4:12	1 Peter 3:12
Colossians 3:16	Colossians 4:2
Joshua 1:8	Ephesians 6:10
1 Peter 1:23	Luke 18:1
Psalm 91:4	James 5:16
Psalm 119:105	Psalm 37:4,5
Psalm 37:23	Philippians 2:13
Colossians 1:9	2 Corinthians 10:5
John 16:13	Psalm 112:7,8

Godly Wisdom in the Affairs of Life

Father, You said if anyone lacks wisdom, let him ask of You, Who giveth to all men liberally, and upbraideth not; and it shall be given him. Therefore, I ask in faith, nothing wavering, to be filled with the knowledge of Your will in all wisdom and spiritual understanding. Today I incline my ear unto wisdom, and apply my heart to understanding so that I might receive that which has been freely given unto me.

In the name of Jesus, I receive skill and godly wisdom and instruction. I discern and comprehend the words of understanding and insight. I receive instruction in wise dealing and the discipline of wise thoughtfulness, righteousness, justice and integrity. Prudence, knowledge, discretion and discernment are given to me. I increase in knowledge. As a person of understanding, I acquire skill and attain to sound counsels [so that I may be able to steer my course rightly].

Wisdom will keep, defend and protect me; I love her and she guards me. I prize Wisdom highly and exalt her; she will bring me to honor because I

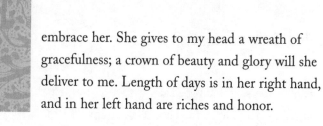
embrace her. She gives to my head a wreath of gracefulness; a crown of beauty and glory will she deliver to me. Length of days is in her right hand, and in her left hand are riches and honor.

Jesus has been made unto me wisdom, and in Him are all the treasures of [divine] wisdom, [of comprehensive insight into the ways and purposes of God], and [all the riches of spiritual] knowledge and enlightenment are stored up and lie hidden. God has hidden away sound and godly wisdom and stored it up for me, for I am the righteousness of God in Christ Jesus.

Therefore, I will walk in paths of uprightness. When I walk, my steps shall not be hampered—my path will be clear and open; and when I run I shall not stumble. I take fast hold of instruction, and do not let her go; I guard her, for she is my life. I let my eyes look right on [with fixed purpose], and my gaze is straight before me. I consider well the path of my feet, and I let all my ways be established and ordered aright.

Father, in the name of Jesus, I look carefully to how I walk! I live purposefully and worthily and accurately, not as unwise and witless, but as a wise—

sensible, intelligent person; making the very most of my time—buying up every opportunity. Amen.

Scripture References

James 1:5,6a	1 Corinthians 1:30
Colossians 1:9b	Colossians 2:3 AMP
Proverbs 2:2	Proverbs 2:7 AMP
Proverbs 1:2-5 AMP	2 Corinthians 5:21
Proverbs 4:6,8,9 AMP	Proverbs 4:11-13,25,26 AMP
Proverbs 3:16 AMP	Ephesians 5:15,16 AMP

The Setting of Proper Priorities

Father, too often I allow urgency to dictate my schedule, and I am asking You to help me establish priorities in my work. I confess my weakness* of procrastination and lack of organization. My desire is to live purposefully and worthily and accurately as a wise, sensible, intelligent person.

You have given me a seven-day week—six days to work and the seventh day to rest. I desire to make the most of the time [buying up each opportunity]. Help me plan my day, and stay focused on my assignments.

In the name of Jesus, I demolish and smash warped philosophies concerning time management, tear down barriers erected against the truth of God, and fit every loose thought, emotion and impulse into the structure of life shaped by Christ. I clear my mind of every obstruction and build a life of obedience into maturity.

Father, You are in charge of my work and my plans. I plan the way I want to live, but You alone make me able to live it. Help me to organize my efforts, schedule my activities and budget my time.

Jesus, You want me to relax. It pleases You when I am not preoccupied with getting, so I can respond to God's giving. I know You, Father God, and how You work. I steep my life in God-reality, God-initiative and God-provisions.

By the grace given me, I will not worry about missing out, and my everyday human concerns will be met. I purpose in my heart to seek (aim at and strive after) first of all Your Kingdom, Lord, and Your righteousness [Your way of doing and being right], and then all these things taken together will be given me besides.

Father, Your Word is my compass, and it helps me see my life as complete in Christ. I cast all my cares, worries and concerns over on You, that I might be well-balanced (temperate, sober of mind), vigilant and cautious at all times.

I tune my ears to the word of wisdom and set my heart on a life of understanding. I make insight my priority.

Father, You sent Jesus that I might have life and have it more abundantly. Help me remember that my relationship with You and with others are more important than anything else. Amen.

Scripture References

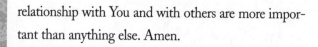

Ephesians 5:15-16 AMP	Genesis 2:2 NIV
2 Corinthians 10:5-6	Proverbs 16:3,9
MESSAGE	MESSAGE
Matthew 11:29	Colossians 2:10
MESSAGE, AMP	1 Peter 5:7-8 AMP
Proverbs 2:3 MESSAGE	John 10:10

If you do not know your strengths and weaknesses, ask the Holy Spirit to reveal them to you. The Lord speaks to us: "My grace is sufficient for you, for power is perfected in weakness" (2 Cor. 12:9 NAS).

Conquering the Thought Life

In the name of Jesus, I take authority over my thought life. Even though I walk (live) in the flesh, I am not carrying on my warfare according to the flesh and using mere human weapons. For the weapons of my warfare are not physical (weapons of flesh and blood), but they are mighty before God for the overthrow and destruction of strongholds. I refute arguments and theories and reasonings and every proud and lofty thing that sets itself up against the (true) knowledge of God; and I lead every thought and purpose away captive into the obedience of Christ, the Messiah, the Anointed One.

With my soul I will bless the Lord with every thought and purpose in life. My mind will not wander out of the presence of God. My life shall glorify the Father—*spirit, soul and body*. I take no account of the evil done to me—I pay no attention to a suffered wrong. It holds no place in my thought life. I am ever ready to believe the best of every person. I gird up the loins of my mind, and I set my mind and keep it set on what is above—the higher things—not on the things that are on the earth.

Whatever is true, whatever is worthy of reverence and is honorable and seemly, whatever is just, whatever is pure, whatever is lovely and lovable, whatever is kind and winsome and gracious, if there is any virtue and excellence, if there is anything worthy of praise, I will think on and weigh and take account of these things—I will fix my mind on them.

I have the mind of Christ, the Messiah, and do hold the thoughts (feelings and purposes) of His heart. In the name of Jesus, I will practice what I have learned and received and heard and seen in Christ and model my way of living on it, and the God of peace—of untroubled, undisturbed wellbeing—will be with me.

In Jesus' name, amen.

Scripture References (AMP)

2 Corinthians 10:3-5   Colossians 3:2

Psalm 103:1   Philippians 4:8

1 Corinthians 6:20   1 Corinthians 2:16

1 Corinthians 13:5b,7a   Philippians 4:9

1 Peter 1:13

Boldness

Father, in the name of Jesus, I am of good courage. I pray that You grant to me that with all *boldness* I speak forth Your Word. I pray that freedom of utterance be given me that I may open my mouth to proclaim *boldly* the mystery of the good news of the Gospel — that I may declare it *boldly* as I ought to do.

Father, I believe I receive that *boldness* now in the name of Jesus. Therefore, I have *boldness* to enter into the Holy of Holies by the blood of Jesus. Because of my faith in Him, I dare to have the *boldness* (courage and confidence) of free access — an unreserved approach to You with freedom and without fear. I can draw fearlessly and confidently and *boldly* near to Your throne of grace and receive mercy and find grace to help in good time for my every need. I am *bold* to pray. I come to the throne of God with my petitions and for others who do not know how to ascend to the throne.

I will be *bold* toward Satan, demons, evil spirits, sickness, disease, and poverty, for Jesus is the Head of all rule and authority — of every angelic principality and power. Disarming those who were ranged against us, Jesus made a *bold* display and public example of them, triumphing over them. I am *bold* to declare that Satan is a defeated foe. Let God arise and His enemies be scattered.

I take comfort and am encouraged and confidently and *boldly* say, "The Lord is my Helper; I will not be seized with alarm — I will not fear or dread or be terrified. What can man do to me?" I dare to proclaim the Word toward heaven, toward hell, and toward earth. I am *bold* as a lion, for I have been made the righteousness of God in Christ Jesus. I am complete in Him! Praise the name of Jesus! Amen.

Scripture References

Psalm 27:14	Hebrews 4:16 AMP
Acts 4:29	Colossians 2:10,15 AMP
Ephesians 6:19,20 AMP	Psalm 68:1
Mark 11:23,24	Hebrews 13:6 AMP
Hebrews 10:19 AMP, KJV	Proverbs 28:1
Ephesians 3:12 AMP	2 Corinthians 5:21

Submitting All to God

Father, You are the Supreme Authority—a God of order. You have instituted other authority structures that will support healthy relationships and maintain harmony. It is my decision to surrender my will to You that I might find protection and dwell in the secret place of the Most High.

Father, thank You for pastors and leaders of the church—those who are submitted to You and are examples to the congregation. I submit to the church elders (the ministers and spiritual guides of the church)— [giving them due respect and yielding to their counsel].

Lord, You know just how rebellious I have been. I ask Your forgiveness for manipulating circumstances and people—for trying to manipulate You to get my own way. May Your will be done in my life, even as it is in heaven.

Father, when I feel that my life is spiraling out of control, I bind my mind to the mind of Christ, and my emotions to the control of the Holy Spirit. I loose my mind from obsessive thought patterns that try to confuse me.

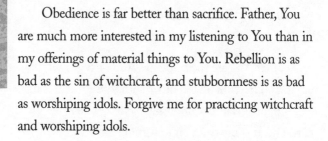

Obedience is far better than sacrifice. Father, You are much more interested in my listening to You than in my offerings of material things to You. Rebellion is as bad as the sin of witchcraft, and stubbornness is as bad as worshiping idols. Forgive me for practicing witchcraft and worshiping idols.

Father, You deserve honesty from the heart; yes, utter sincerity and truthfulness. Oh, give me this wisdom. Sprinkle me with the cleansing blood, and I shall be clean again. Wash me, and I shall be whiter than snow. You have rescued me from the dominion of darkness and brought me into the Kingdom of the Son You love, in Whom I have redemption, the forgiveness of sins.

Lord, I want to follow You. I am putting aside my own desires and conveniences. I yield my desires that are not in Your plan for me. Even in the midst of my fear I surrender and entrust my future to You. I choose to take up my cross and follow You [cleave steadfastly to You, conforming wholly to Your example in living and, if need be, in dying also]. I desire to lose my [lower life] on Your account that I might find it [the higher life].

Father, You gave Jesus to be my Example. He has returned to You, Father, and has sent the Holy Spirit to be my Helper and Guide. In this world there are temptations, trials and tribulations; but Jesus has overcome the world, and I am of good cheer.

Jesus is my Lord. I choose to become His servant. He calls me His friend.

Lord, help me to walk through the process of surrendering my all to You. I exchange rebellion and stubbornness for a willing and obedient heart—when I refuse to listen, anoint my ears to hear; when I am blinded by my own desires, open my eyes to see.

I belong to Jesus Christ, the Anointed One Who breaks down and destroys every yoke of bondage. In His name and in obedience to Your will, Father, I submit to the control and direction of the Holy Spirit Whom You have sent to live in me. I am Your child. All to You I surrender. I am an overcomer by the blood of the Lamb and by the word of my testimony!

In Jesus' name I pray, amen.

Scripture References

1 Corinthians 14:33	Psalm 51:6,7 TLB
1 Timothy 2:2	Colossians 1:13,14 NIV
Psalm 91:1	Matthew 10:38,39 AMP
1 Peter 5:5 AMP	John 16:33
Matthew 6:10	John 15:15
James 4:7	Revelation 12:11
1 Samuel 15:22,23 TLB	

Casting Down Imaginations

Father, though I live in the world, I do not wage war as the world does. The weapons I fight with are not the weapons of the world. On the contrary, they have divine power to demolish strongholds. I demolish arguments and every pretension that sets itself up against the knowledge of You, and I take captive every thought to make it obedient to Christ.

In the name of Jesus, I ask You, Father, to bless those who have despitefully used me. Whenever I feel afraid, I will trust in You. When I feel miserable, I will express thanksgiving; and when I feel that life is unfair, I will remember that You are more than enough.

When I feel ashamed, help me to remember that I no longer have to be afraid; I will not suffer shame. I am delivered from the fear of disgrace; I will not be humiliated. I relinquish the shame of my youth.

It is well with my soul, for You have redeemed me. You have called me by name.

I am in Your will for my life at this time. I am being transformed through the renewing of my mind. I am able to test and approve [for myself] what Your will is—Your good and acceptable and perfect will.

You have good things reserved for my future. All my needs will be met according to Your riches in glory. I will replace worry for my family with asking You to protect and care for them.

You are love, and perfect love casts out fear.

In Jesus' name, amen.

Scripture References

2 Corinthians 10:3-5 NIV	Romans 12:2 AMP
Luke 6:28	Jeremiah 29:11 AMP
Isaiah 54:4 NIV	Philippians 4:19
Isaiah 43:1	1 Peter 5:7
Romans 12:2	1 John 4:8,18

Walking in Humility

Father, I clothe myself with humility [as the garb of a servant, so that its covering cannot possibly be stripped from me]. I renounce pride and arrogance. Father, You give grace to the humble. Therefore I humble myself under Your mighty hand, that in due time You may exalt me.

In the name of Jesus, I cast the whole of my care [all my anxieties, all my worries, all my concerns for my future, once and for all] on You, for You care for me affectionately and care about me watchfully. I expect a life of victory and awesome deeds because my actions are done on behalf of a spirit humbly submitted to Your truth and righteousness.

Father, in the name of Jesus, I refuse to be wise in my own eyes; but I choose to fear You and shun evil. This will bring health to my body and nourishment to my bones.

Father, I humble myself and submit to Your Word that exposes, sifts, analyzes and judges the very thoughts and purposes of my heart. I test my own

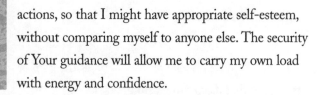
actions, so that I might have appropriate self-esteem, without comparing myself to anyone else. The security of Your guidance will allow me to carry my own load with energy and confidence.

I listen carefully and hear what is being said to me. I incline my ear to wisdom and apply my heart to understanding and insight. Humility and fear of You bring wealth and honor and life.

Father, I hide Your Word in my heart that I might not sin against You. As one of Your chosen people, holy and dearly loved, I clothe myself with compassion, kindness, humility, gentleness and patience. I bear with others and forgive whatever grievances I may have against anyone. I forgive as You forgave me. And over all these virtues I put on love, which binds them all together in perfect unity. I let the peace of Christ rule in my heart, and I am thankful for Your grace and the power of the Holy Spirit.

Father, may Your will be done on earth in my life as it is in heaven.

In Jesus' name, amen.

Scripture References

1 Peter 5:5-7 AMP

Proverbs 3:7,8 NIV

Hebrews 4:12 AMP

Galatians 6:4,5 NIV

Proverbs 2:2 NIV

Proverbs 22:4 NIV

Psalm 119:11

Colossians 3:12-15 NIV

Matthew 6:10 NIV

To Watch What You Say

Father, today I make a commitment to You in the name of Jesus. I turn from speaking idle words and foolishly talking things that are contrary to my true desire to myself and toward others. Your Word says that the tongue defiles, that the tongue sets on fire the course of nature, that the tongue is set on fire of hell.

In the name of Jesus, I submit to godly wisdom that I might learn to control my tongue. I am determined that hell will not set my tongue on fire. I renounce, reject, and repent of every word that has ever proceeded out of my mouth against You, God, and Your operation. I cancel its power and dedicate my mouth to speak excellent and right things. My mouth shall utter truth.

Because I am the righteousness of God in Christ Jesus, I set the course of my life for obedience, for abundance, for wisdom, for health, and for joy. Set a guard over my mouth, O Lord; keep watch over the door of my lips. Then the words of my mouth and my deeds shall show forth Your righteousness and Your salvation all of my days. I purpose to guard my mouth and my tongue that I might keep myself from calamity.

Father, Your Words are top priority to me. They are spirit and life. I let the Word dwell in me richly in all wisdom. The ability of God is released within me by the words of my mouth and by the Word of God. I speak Your Words out of my mouth. They are alive in me. You are alive and working in me. So, I can boldly say that my words are words of faith, words of power, words of love, and words of life. They produce good things in my life and in the lives of others because I choose Your Words for my lips, and Your will for my life, in Jesus' name. Amen.

Scripture References

Ephesians 5:4	Proverbs 21:23
2 Timothy 2:16	Ephesians 4:27
James 3:6	James 1:6
Proverbs 8:6,7	John 6:63
2 Corinthians 5:21	Colossians 3:16
Proverbs 4:23	Philemon 6

To Obtain and Maintain Godly Character

Father, I desire to receive wisdom and discipline. I ask for the ability to understand words of insight. By Your grace, I am acquiring a disciplined and prudent life, doing what is right and just and fair.

Thank You for giving me prudence, knowledge and discretion. As a wise person I listen and add to my learning, and as a discerning person I accept guidance [so that I may be able to steer my course rightly].

Thank You that I understand proverbs and parables, the sayings and riddles of the wise.

In Jesus' name I pray, amen.

Scripture References

Proverbs 1:2-7 NIV   Proverbs 1:5 AMP

Letting Go of the Past

Father, I realize my helplessness in saving myself, and I glory in what Christ Jesus has done for me. I let go—put aside all past sources of my confidence—counting them worth less than nothing, in order that I may experience Christ and become one with Him.

Lord, I have received Your Son, and He has given me the authority (power, privilege and right) to become Your child.

I unfold my past and put into proper perspective those things that are behind. I have been crucified with Christ; and I no longer live, but Christ lives in me. The life I live in the body, I live by faith in the Son of God, Who loved me and gave Himself for me. I trust in You, Lord, with all my heart and lean not on my own understanding. In all my ways I acknowledge You, and You will make my paths straight.

I want to know Christ and the power of His resurrection and the fellowship of sharing in His sufferings, becoming like Him in His death, and so, somehow, to attain to the resurrection from the dead. So, whatever it takes, I will be one who lives in the fresh newness of life of those who are alive from the dead.

I don't mean to say that I am perfect. I haven't learned all I should even yet, but I keep working toward that day when I will finally be all that Christ saved me for and wants me to be.

I am bringing all my energies to bear on this one thing: Regardless of my past I look forward to what lies ahead. I strain to reach the end of the race and receive the prize for which You are calling me up to heaven because of what Christ Jesus did for me.

In His name I pray, amen.

Scripture References

Philippians 3:7-9 TLB   Proverbs 3:5,6 NIV

John 1:12 AMP   Philippians 3:10,11 NIV

Psalm 32:5 AMP   Romans 6:4

Philippians 3:13   Philippians 3:12-14 TLB

Galatians 2:20 NIV

Overcoming Discouragement

Introduction

Moses returned to the Lord and said, "O Lord, why have you brought trouble upon this people? Is this why you sent me? Ever since I went to Pharaoh to speak in your name, he has brought trouble upon this people, and you have not rescued your people at all."

Exodus 5:22,23 NIV

Here in this passage, we find Moses discouraged, complaining to God.

It is important that we approach God with integrity in an attitude of humility. Because we fear making a negative confession, we sometimes cross the line of honesty into the line of denial and delusion.

Let's be honest. God already knows what we are feeling. He can handle our anger, complaints and disappointments. He understands us. He is aware of our human frailties (Ps. 103:14) and can be touched with the feelings of our infirmities (Heb. 4:15).

Whether your "trouble" is a business failure, aban-
donment, depression, mental disorder, chemical imbal-
ance, oppression, a marriage problem, a child who is in a
strange land of drugs and alcohol, financial disaster or
anything else, the following prayer is for you.

Sometimes when you are in the midst of discouragement it is difficult to remember that you have ever
known any Scripture. I admonish you to read this prayer
aloud until you recognize the reality of God's Word in
your spirit, soul and body. Remember, God is watching
over His Word to perform it (Jer. 1:12 AMP). He will
perfect that which concerns you (Ps. 138:8).

Prayer

Lord, I have exhausted all my possibilities for
changing my situation and circumstances and have
found that I am powerless to change. I believe; help me
overcome my unbelief. All things are not possible with
man, but all things are possible with You. I humble
myself before You, and You will lift me up.

I have a great High Priest Who has gone through
the heavens, Jesus Your Son, and I hold firmly to the

faith I profess. My High Priest is able to sympathize with my weaknesses. He was tempted in every way, just as I am—yet was without sin. I approach Your throne of grace with confidence, so that I may receive mercy and find grace to help me in my time of need.

In the face of discouragement, disappointment and anger, I choose to believe that Your Word to Moses is Your Word to me. You are mighty to deliver. Because of Your mighty hand, You will drive out the forces that have set themselves up against me. You are the Lord, Yahweh, the Promise-Keeper, the Almighty One. You appeared to Abraham, to Isaac and to Jacob and established Your covenant with them.

Father, I believe that You have heard my groaning, my cries. I will live to see Your promises of deliverance fulfilled in my life. You have not forgotten one word of Your promise; You are a Covenant-Keeper.

It is You Who will bring me out from under the yoke of bondage and free me from being a slave to _____. You have redeemed me with an outstretched arm and with mighty acts of judgment. You have taken me as Your own, and You are my God.

You are a Father to me. You have delivered me from the past that has held me in bondage and translated me into the Kingdom of love, peace, joy and righteousness. I will no longer settle for the pain of the past. Where sin abounds, grace does much more abound.

Father, what You have promised, I will go and possess, in the name of Jesus. I am willing to take the chance, to take the risk, to get back into the good fight of faith. It is with patient endurance and steady and active persistence that I run the race, the appointed course that is set before me. I rebuke the spirit of fear for I am established in righteousness. Oppression and destruction shall not come near me. Behold, they may gather together and stir up strife, but it is not from You, Father. Whoever stirs up strife against me shall fall and surrender to me. I am more than a conqueror through Him Who loves me.

In His name I pray, amen.

Scripture References

*(This prayer is based on Exodus 5:22–6:11
and includes other verses where applicable.)*

Mark 9:24 NIV	Deuteronomy 26:8
Luke 18:27	Colossians 1:13
1 Peter 5:6 NIV	Romans 5:20
Hebrews 4:14-16 NIV	1 Timothy 6:12
Exodus 6:3,4 AMP	Hebrews 12:1 AMP
Genesis 49:22-26 AMP	Isaiah 54:14-16
1 Kings 8:56	Romans 8:37

Strength To Overcome Cares and Burdens

Why are you cast down, O my inner self? And why should you moan over me and be disquieted within me?

Father, You set Yourself against the proud and haughty, but give grace [continually] unto the humble. I submit myself therefore to You, God. In the name of Jesus, I resist the devil, and he will flee from me. I resist the cares of the world which try to pressure me daily. Except the Lord builds the house, they labor in vain who build it.

Jesus, I come to You, for I labor and am heavy laden and overburdened, and You cause me to rest—You will ease and relieve and refresh my soul.

I take Your yoke upon me, and I learn of You; for You are gentle (meek) and humble (lowly) in heart, and I will find rest—relief, ease and refreshment and recreation and blessed quiet—for my soul. For Your yoke is wholesome *(easy)*—not harsh, hard, sharp or pressing, but comfortable, gracious and pleasant; and Your burden is light and easy to be borne.

I cast my burden on You, Lord, [releasing the weight of it] and You will sustain me; I thank You that You will never allow me, the [consistently] righteous, to be moved—made to slip, fall or fail.

In the name of Jesus, I withstand the devil. I am firm in my faith [against his onset]—rooted, established, strong, immovable and determined. I cease from [the weariness and pain] of human labor and am zealous and exert myself and strive diligently to enter into the rest [of God]—to know and experience it for myself.

Father, I thank You that Your presence goes with me, and that You give me rest. I am still and rest in You, Lord; I wait for You and patiently stay myself upon You. I will not fret myself, nor shall I let my heart be troubled, neither shall I let it be afraid. I hope in You, God, and wait expectantly for You; for I shall yet praise You, for You are the Help of my countenance, and my God.

In Jesus' name, amen.

Scripture References (AMP)

Psalm 42:11a   Hebrews 4:10b,11

James 4:6,7

Psalm 127:1a

Matthew 11:28-30

Psalm 55:22

1 Peter 5:9a

Exodus 33:14

Psalm 37:7

John 14:27b

Psalm 42:11b

Victory Over Pride

Father, Your Word says that You hate a proud look, that You resist the proud but give grace to the humble. I submit myself therefore to You, God. In the name of Jesus, I resist the devil, and he will flee from me. I renounce every manifestation of pride in my life as sin; I repent and turn from it.

As an act of faith, I clothe myself with humility and receive Your grace. I humble myself under Your mighty hand, Lord, that You may exalt me in due time. I refuse to exalt myself. I do not think of myself more highly than I ought; I do not have an exaggerated opinion of my own importance, but rate my ability with sober judgment, according to the degree of faith apportioned to me.

Proverbs 11:2 says, **When pride cometh, then cometh shame: but with the lowly is wisdom.** Father, I set myself to resist pride when it comes. My desire is to be counted among the lowly, so I take on the attitude of a servant.

Father, thank You that You dwell with him who is of a contrite and humble spirit. You revive the spirit of the humble and revive the heart of the contrite ones. Thank You that the reward of humility and the reverent and worshipful fear of the Lord is riches and honor and life.

In Jesus' name I pray, amen.

Scripture References

Proverbs 6:16

James 4:6,7

Proverbs 21:4

1 Peter 5:5,6

Romans 12:3 AMP

Proverbs 11:2

Matthew 23:11

Isaiah 57:15

Proverbs 22:4 AMP

Victory in a Healthy Lifestyle

Father, I am Your child and Jesus is Lord over my spirit, soul and body. I praise You because I am fearfully and wonderfully made; Your works are wonderful, I know that full well.

Lord, thank You for declaring Your plans for me — plans to prosper me and not to harm me, plans to give me hope and a future. I choose to renew my mind to Your plans for a healthy lifestyle. You have abounded toward me in all prudence and wisdom. Therefore I give thought to my steps. Teach me knowledge and good judgement.

My body is for the Lord. So here's what I want to do with Your help, Father-God. I choose to take my everyday, ordinary life—my sleeping, eating, going-to-work, and walking-around life—and place it before You as an offering. Embracing what You do for me is the best thing I can do for You.

Christ the Messiah will be magnified and receive glory and praise in this body of mine and will be boldly exalted in my person. Thank you, Father, in Jesus name! Hallelujah! Amen.

Scripture References

Psalm 139:14	Psalms 119:66
Jeremiah 29:11	Romans 12:1 MESSAGE
Proverbs 14:15	Philippians 1:20 AMP

Victory Over Fear

Father, when I am afraid, I will put my confidence in You. Yes, I will trust Your promises. And since I trust You, what can mere man do to me?

You have not given me a spirit of timidity, but of power and love and discipline (sound judgement). Therefore I am not ashamed of the testimony of my Lord. I have not received a spirit of slavery leading to fear again, but I have received a spirit of adoption as a son by which I cry out, "Abba! Father!"

Jesus, You delivered me who through fear of death had been living all my life as a slave to constant dread. I receive the gift You left to me – peace of mind and heart! And the peace You give isn't fragile like the peace the world gives. I cast away troubled thoughts and I choose not to be afraid. I believe in God, I believe also in You.

Lord, You are my light and my salvation, You protect me from danger – whom shall I fear? When evil men come to destroy me, they will stumble and fall! Yes, though a might army marches against me, my heart shall know no fear! I am confident that You will save me.

Thank you, Holy Spirit for bringing these things to my remembrance when I am tempted to be afraid. I will trust in my God. In the name of Jesus, I pray.

Scripture References

Psalm 56:3-5 TLB	Hebrews 2:15 TLB
2 Timothy 1:7-8 NAS	John 14:1,17 TLB
Romans 8:15 NAS	Psalm 27:1-3 TLB

Health and Healing

Father, in the name of Jesus, I come before You asking You to heal me. It is written that the prayer of faith will save the sick, and the Lord will raise him up. And if I have committed sins, I will be forgiven. I let go of all unforgiveness, resentment, anger and bad feelings toward anyone.

My body is the temple of the Holy Spirit, and I desire to be in good health. I seek truth that will make me free – both spiritual and natural *(good eating habits, medications if necessary, and appropriate rest and exercise).* You bought me at a price, and I desire to glorify You in my spirit and my body – they both belong to You.

Thank you, Father, for sending Your Word to heal me and deliver me from all my destructions. Jesus, You are the Word who became flesh and dwelt among us. You bore my griefs (pains) and carried my sorrows (sickness). You were pierced through for my transgressions, crushed for my iniquities, the chastening for my well being fell upon You, and by Your scourging I am healed.

Father, I give attention to Your words, and incline my ear to Your sayings. I will not let them depart from my sight, but keep them in the midst of my heart. For they are my life and health to my whole body.

Since the Spirit of Him who raised Jesus from the dead dwells in me, He who raised Christ from the dead will also give life to my mortal body through His Spirit who dwells in me.

Thank you that I will prosper and be in health even as my soul prospers. Amen.

Scripture References

James 5:15 NKJ

1 Corinthians 6:19-20

Psalm 107:20

John 1:14

Isaiah 53:4-5 NAS

Proverbs 4:21-22 NAS

Psalm 103:3-5 NAS

Romans 8:11 NKJ

3 John 2

Safety

Father, in the name of Jesus, I thank You that You watch over Your Word to perform it. I thank You that I dwell in the secret place of the Most High and that I remain stable and fixed under the shadow of the Almighty Whose power no foe can withstand.

Father, You are my Refuge and my Fortress. *No evil shall befall me—no accident shall overtake me—nor any plague or calamity come near my home.* You give Your angels special charge over me, to accompany and defend and preserve me in all my ways of obedience and service. They are encamped around about me.

Father, You are my Confidence, firm and strong. You keep my foot from being caught in a trap or hidden danger. Father, You give me safety and ease me—*Jesus is my safety!*

Traveling—As I go, I say, "Let me pass over to the other side," and I have what I say. I walk on my way securely and in confident trust, for my heart and mind are firmly fixed and stayed on You, and I am kept in perfect peace.

Sleeping—Father, I sing for joy upon my bed because You sustain me. In peace I lie down and sleep, for You alone, Lord, make me dwell in safety. I lie down, and I am not afraid. My sleep is sweet, for You give blessings to me in sleep. Thank You, Father, in Jesus' name. Amen.

Continue to feast and meditate upon all of Psalm 91 for yourself and your loved ones!

Scripture References

Jeremiah 1:12	Proverbs 3:23 AMP
Psalm 91:1,2 AMP	Psalm 112:7
Psalm 91:10 AMP	Isaiah 26:3
Psalm 91:11 AMP	Psalm 149:5
Psalm 34:7	Psalm 3:5
Proverbs 3:26 AMP	Psalm 4:8 AMP
Isaiah 49:25	Proverbs 3:24
Mark 4:35	Psalm 127:2

Handling the Day of Trouble or Calamity

Introduction

During a time of trouble or calamity, it is sometimes difficult to remember the promises of God. The
pressures of the moment may seem overwhelming. At
such times, it is often helpful to read, meditate on and
pray the entire chapter of Psalm 91.

It may be that during a stressful time you will find
this entire prayer too long. If so, draw from the
Scriptures included in the following prayer. You may
find yourself praying one paragraph or reading it aloud
to yourself or to your family and friends.

I also encourage you to meditate on this prayer
during good times.

At all times, remember that faith comes by hearing,
and hearing by the Word of God (Rom. 10:17).

Prayer

Father, I come to You in the name of Jesus,
acknowledging You as my Refuge and High Tower. You

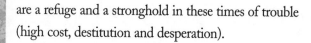
are a refuge and a stronghold in these times of trouble
(high cost, destitution and desperation).

In the day of trouble, You will hide me in Your
shelter; in the secret place of Your tent will You hide me;
You will set me high upon a rock. And now shall my
head be lifted up above my enemies round about me; in
Your tent I will offer sacrifices and shouting of joy; I will
sing, yes, I will sing praises to You, O Lord. Hear, O
Lord, when I cry aloud; have mercy and be gracious to
me and answer me!

On the authority of Your Word, I declare that I
have been made the righteousness of God in Christ
Jesus. When I cry for help, You, Lord, hear me and
deliver me out of all my distress and troubles. You are
close to me, for I am of a broken heart, and You save
such as are crushed with sorrow for sin and are humbly
and thoroughly penitent. Lord, many are the evils that
confront me, but You deliver me out of them all.

Thank You for being merciful and gracious to me,
O God, for my soul takes refuge and finds shelter and
confidence in You; yes, in the shadow of Your wings I
take refuge and am confident until calamities and

destructive storms are passed. You perform on my behalf and reward me. You bring to pass Your purposes for me, and surely You complete them!

Father, You are my Refuge and Strength [might and impenetrable to temptation], a very present and well-proved help in trouble.

Lord, You have given and bequeathed to me Your peace. By Your grace I will not let my heart be troubled; neither will I let it be afraid. With the help of the Holy Spirit I will [stop allowing myself to be agitated and disturbed; and I refuse to permit myself to be fearful and intimidated and cowardly and unsettled].

By faith, I respond to these troubles and calamities: [I am full of joy now!] I exult and triumph in my troubles and rejoice in my sufferings, knowing that pressure and affliction and hardship produce patient and unswerving endurance. And endurance (fortitude) develops maturity of character (approved faith and tried integrity). And character [of this sort] produces [the habit of] joyful and confident hope of eternal salvation. Such hope never disappoints or deludes or shames me,

for Your love has been poured out in my heart through the Holy Spirit Who has been given to me.

In Jesus' name, amen.

Scripture References

Psalm 9:9 AMP	Psalm 57:1,2 AMP
Psalm 27:5-7 AMP	Psalm 46:1 AMP
2 Corinthians 5:21	John 14:27 AMP
Psalm 34:17-20 AMP	Romans 5:3-5 AMP

Peaceful Sleep

Father, thank You for peaceful sleep, and Your angels that encamp around us who fear You. You deliver us, and keep us safe. The angels excel in strength, do Your Word, and heed the voice of Your Word. You give Your angels charge over me, to keep me in all my ways.

I bring every thought, every imagination and every dream into the captivity and obedience of Jesus Christ. Father, I thank You that even as I sleep my heart counsels me and reveals to me Your purpose and plan. Thank You for sweet sleep, for You promised Your beloved sweet sleep. Therefore, my heart is glad, and my spirit rejoices. My body and soul rest and confidently dwell in safety. Amen.

Scripture References

Proverbs 3:24   2 Corinthians 10:5

Psalm 34:7   Psalm 92:11

Psalm 103:20

Prosperity

Father, I come to You in the name of Jesus, concerning my financial situation. You are a very present help in trouble, and You are more than enough. Your word declares that You shall supply all my need according to Your riches in glory by Christ Jesus.

(If you have not been giving tithes and offerings include the statement of repentance in your prayer.) Forgive me for robbing You in tithes and offerings. I repent, and purpose to bring all my tithes into the storehouse that there may be food in Your house. Thank You for wise financial counselors and teachers who are teaching me the principles of good stewardship.

Lord of hosts, You said, "Try me now in this, and You will open the windows of heaven and pour out for me such blessing that there will not be room enough to receive it." You will rebuke the devourer for my sake, and my heart is filled with thanksgiving.

Lord, my God, I shall remember that it is You who gives me the power to get wealth that You may establish

Your covenant. In the name of Jesus, I worship You only, and I will have no others gods before me.

You are able to make all grace – every favor and earthly blessing – come to me in abundance, so that I am always, and in all circumstances furnished in abundance for every good work and charitable donation. Amen.

Scripture References

Psalm 56:1

Philippians 4:19

Malachi 3: 8-12

Deuteronomy 8:18-19

2 Corinthians 9:8 AMP

Pleading the Blood of Jesus

I
Morning Prayer[1]

Father, I come in the name of Jesus to plead His blood on my life and on all that belongs to me, and on all that over which You have made me a steward.

I plead the blood of Jesus on the portals of my mind, my body (the temple of the Holy Spirit), my emotions and my will. I believe that I am protected by the blood of the Lamb that gives me access to the Holy of Holies.

I plead the blood on my children, my grandchildren and their children, and on all those whom You have given me in this life.

Lord, You have said that the life of the flesh is in the blood. Thank You for this blood that has cleansed me from sin and sealed the New Covenant of which I am a partaker.

In Jesus' name, amen.

---

[1]Based on a prayer written by Joyce Meyer in *The Word, the Name and the Blood* (Tulsa: Harrison House, 1995).

Scripture References

Exodus 12:7,13	Leviticus 17:11
1 Corinthians 6:19	1 John 1:7
Hebrews 9:6-14	Hebrews 13:20 AMP

II
Evening Prayer [2]

Father, as I lie down to sleep, I plead the blood of Jesus upon my life—within me, around me and between me and all evil and the author of evil.

In Jesus' name, amen.

---

[2]Based on a prayer written by Mrs. C. Nuzum as recorded by Billye Brim in *The Blood and the Glory* (Tulsa: Harrison House, 1995).

In Court Cases

Father, in the name of Jesus, it is written in Your Word to call on You and You will answer me and show me great and mighty things. I put You in remembrance of Your Word and thank You that You watch over it to perform it.

I say that no weapon formed against me shall prosper and any tongue that rises against me in judgment I shall show to be in the wrong. This peace, security and triumph over opposition is my inheritance as Your child. This is the righteousness which I obtain from You, Father, which You impart to me as my justification. I am far from even the thought of destruction, for I shall not fear, and terror shall not come near me.

Father, You say You will establish me to the end—keep me steadfast, give me strength and guarantee my vindication; that is, be my warrant against all accusation or indictment. Father, You contend with those who contend with me, and You perfect that which concerns me. I dwell in the secret place of the Most High, and this secret place hides me from the strife of tongues, for a false witness who breathes out lies is an abomination to You.

I am a true witness, and all my words are upright and in right standing with You, Father. By my long forbearing and calmness of spirit the judge is persuaded, and my soft speech breaks down the most bonelike resistance. Therefore, I am not anxious beforehand how I shall reply in defense or what I am to say, for the Holy Spirit teaches me *in that very hour* and moment what I ought to say to those in the outside world. My speech is seasoned with salt.

As a child of the light, I enforce the triumphant victory of my Lord Jesus Christ in this situation knowing that all of heaven is backing me. I am strong in You, Lord, and in the power of Your might. Thank You for the shield of faith that quenches every fiery dart of the enemy. I am increasing in wisdom and in stature and years, and in favor with You, Father and with man. Praise the Lord! Amen.

Scripture References

Jeremiah 33:3

Jeremiah 1:12 AMP

Isaiah 43:26 AMP

Isaiah 54:17 AMP

Isaiah 54:14 AMP

1 Corinthians 1:8 AMP

Isaiah 49:25

Psalm 138:8

Psalm 91:1

Psalm 31:20

Proverbs 6:19

Proverbs 14:25

Proverbs 8:8 AMP

Proverbs 25:15 AMP

Luke 12:11,12 AMP

Colossians 4:6

Matthew 18:18

Ephesians 6:10,16

Luke 2:52

To Receive the Infilling of the Holy Spirit

My Heavenly Father, I am Your child, for I believe in my heart that Jesus has been raised from the dead and I have confessed Him as my Lord.

Jesus said, "How much more shall your heavenly Father give the Holy Spirit to those who ask Him." I ask You now in the name of Jesus to fill me with the Holy Spirit. I step into the fullness and power that I desire in the name of Jesus. I confess that I am a Spirit-filled Christian. As I yield my vocal organs, I expect to speak in tongues, for the Spirit gives me utterance in the name of Jesus. Praise the Lord! Amen.

Scripture References

John 14:16,17	Acts 10:44-46
Luke 11:13	Acts 19:2,5,6
Acts 1:8a	1 Corinthians 14:2-15
Acts 2:4	1 Corinthians 14:18,27
Acts 2:32,33,39	Ephesians 6:18
Acts 8:12-17	Jude 1:20

Part Two

PRAYERS FOR RELATIONSHIPS

Developing Healthy Friendships

Father, help me to meet new friends—friends who will encourage me. May I find in these friendships the companionship and fellowship You have ordained for me. I know that You are my Source of love, companionship and friendship. Your love and friendship are expressed through my relationship with You and members of the Body of Christ.

According to Proverbs 27:17 CEV, iron sharpens iron, so friends sharpen the minds of each other. As we learn from each other, may we find a worthy purpose in our relationship. Keep me well balanced in my friendships, so that I will always please You rather than pleasing other people.

I ask for divine connections—good friendships ordained by You. Thank You for the courage and grace to let go of detrimental friendships. I ask and receive, by faith, discernment for developing healthy relationships. Your Word says that two are better than one, because if one falls, there will be someone to lift that person up.

Father, You know the hearts of people, so I won't be deceived by outward appearances. Bad friendships corrupt good morals. Thank You for quality friends who help me build a stronger character and draw me closer to You. Help me be a friend to others and to love my friends at all times. I will laugh with those who laugh, I will rejoice with those who rejoice, and I will weep with those who weep. Teach me what I need to know to be a quality friend.

Develop in me a fun personality and a good sense of humor. Help me to relax around people and to be myself—the person You created me to be. Instruct my heart and mold my character, that I may be faithful and trustworthy over the friendships You are sending into my life.

Father, Your Son Jesus is my Best Friend. He is a friend Who sticks closer than a brother. He defined the standard when He said in John 15:13, **Greater love hath no man than this, that a man lay down his life for his friends.**

Thank You, Lord, that I can entrust myself and my need for friends into Your keeping. I submit to the leadership of the Holy Spirit, in the name of Jesus. Amen.

Scripture References

Proverbs 13:20 NIV   James 1:17 NIV

Ephesians 5:30 NIV   Proverbs 17:17

Philippians 2:2,3 NIV   Romans 12:15

Psalm 84:11 NIV   Proverbs 18:24

Ecclesiastes 4:9,10 NIV Psalm 37:4,5 NIV

1 Corinthians 15:33 AMP

This prayer is composed of Scriptures and writings taken from
"Meeting New Friends," *Prayers That Avail Much for Teens!*
(Tulsa: Harrison House, 1991), pp. 50-52.

Maintaining Good Relations

Father, in the name of Jesus, I will not withhold good from those to whom it is due [its rightful owners], when it is in the power of my hand to do it. I will render to all men their dues. I will [pay] taxes to whom taxes are due, revenue to whom revenue is due, respect to whom respect is due and honor to whom honor is due.

I will not lose heart and grow weary and faint in acting nobly and doing nobly and right, for in due season I shall reap, if I do not loosen and relax my courage and faint. So then, as occasion and opportunity open up to me, I will do good [morally] to all people [not only being useful or profitable to them, but also doing what is for their spiritual good and advantage]. I am mindful to be a blessing, especially to those of the household of faith [those who belong to God's family with me, the believers].

I will not contend with a man for no reason—when he has done me no wrong. If possible, as far as it depends on me, I purpose to live at peace with everyone. Amen.

Scripture References

Proverbs 3:27 AMP

Proverbs 3:30 AMP

Romans 13:7 AMP

Romans 12:18 AMP

Galatians 6:9,10 AMP

Improving Communication Skills

Introduction

Lack of communication skills is one of the greatest hindrances to healthy relationships. Most of the time when we pray, we are seeking change. We cannot change others, but we can submit to the constant ministry of transformation by the Holy Spirit (Rom. 12:1,2).

Prayer prepares us for change. Change produces change, which may be uncomfortable. If we will move through the discomfort, God will work with us, leading us out of our self-developed defense mechanisms into a place of victory. In this place He heals our brokenness, becomes our defense and our vindication. We are enabled to submit to the Champion of our salvation, which we are working out with fear and trembling (Phil. 2:12).

Adults who grew up in judgmental, critical homes where they were never allowed to express themselves sometimes carry much hurt and anger into their rela-tionships. Often they were not permitted to have their

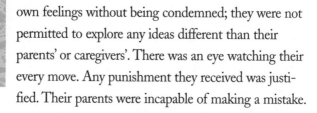
own feelings without being condemned; they were not permitted to explore any ideas different than their parents' or caregivers'. There was an eye watching their every move. Any punishment they received was justified. Their parents were incapable of making a mistake.

Adult children of religiously rigid environments were led to believe that any slip, error in judgment, or mistake was a sin that would send them straight to hell; the parents' religious doctrine was the only way to heaven, and to deviate from it would lead to destruction. Forgiveness could be attained only after much sorrow, penance, and retribution. Death before the completion of repentance led to an eternity in hell.

People raised in such oppressive home environments were never allowed to find themselves or to travel their own individual spiritual journeys leading to truth. The head of the home, usually the father, was considered God in the flesh. Conflict resolution was never taught or practiced. Whatever the head of the household said was law — and disobedience to his law was not discussed, but beaten out of the child. The wife was subservient and was not allowed to question the dictates of the husband.

When these adults marry, they often feel that they have finally found a platform from which to express themselves. They have escaped a place of abiding fear, constant condemnation, and continual criticism. Having no communication skills, they often have difficulty expressing themselves properly. When anyone disagrees with them, they tend to react as they were taught. Only now, the marriage partner or friend does not submit to dogmatic, manipulative words. Frustration develops. The adult child seeks to make himself or herself understood, resulting in more frustration. Anger is fed, and the individual continues to be in bondage to the idea that he or she should never have been born. The person either retreats to a silent corner, refusing to talk, or uses words to build walls of defense — shutting others out. He or she resides inside emotional isolation, attempting to remove himself or herself from more hurt and criticism.

There is a way of escape. God sent His Word to heal us and to deliver us from all our destructions (Ps. 107:20). We must determine to listen, to learn, and to change with the help of the Holy Spirit — our Teacher, our Guide, and our Intercessor. The anointing is upon

Jesus to bind up and heal our emotional wounds (Luke 4:18). His anointing destroys every yoke of bondage (Isa. 10:27), setting the captives free.

Prayer

Father, I am Your child. Jesus said that if I pray to You in secret, You will reward me openly.

Father, I desire with all my heart to walk in love, but I am ever sabotaging my own efforts and failing in my relationships. I know that without faith it is impossible to please and be satisfactory to You. I am coming near to You, believing that You exist and that You are the Rewarder of those who earnestly and diligently seek You.

Show "me" to me. Uncover me — bring everything to the light. When anything is exposed and reproved by the light, it is made visible and clear; and where everything is visible and clear, there is light.

Heal the past wounds and hurts that have controlled my behavior and my speech. Teach me to guard my heart with all diligence, for out of it flow the very issues of life. Teach me to speak the truth in love in my home, in my church, with my friends, and in all my relationships. Also, help me to realize that others have a right to express themselves. Help me to make room for their ideas and their opinions, even when they are different than mine.

Words are powerful. The power of life and death is in the tongue, and You said that I would eat the fruit of it.

Father, I realize that words can be creative or destructive. A word out of my mouth may seem of no account, but it can accomplish nearly anything — or destroy it! A careless or wrongly placed word out of my mouth can set off a forest fire. By my speech I can ruin the world, turn harmony to chaos, throw mud on a reputation, send the whole world up in smoke, and go up in smoke with it — smoke right from the pit of hell. This is scary!

Father, forgive me for speaking curses. I reacted out of past hurts and unresolved anger. At times I am dogmatic, even boasting that I am wise; sometimes unknowingly I have twisted the truth to make myself sound wise; at times I have tried to look better than

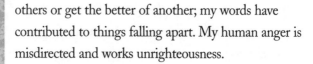
others or get the better of another; my words have
contributed to things falling apart. My human anger is
misdirected and works unrighteousness.

Father, forgive me. I cannot change myself, but I
am willing to change and walk in the wisdom that is
from above.

Father, I submit to that wisdom from above that
begins with a holy life and is characterized by getting
along with others. It is gentle and reasonable, overflowing with mercy and blessings, not hot one day and cold
the next, not two-faced. Use me as Your instrument to
develop a healthy, robust community that lives right
with You. I will enjoy its results only if I do the hard
work of getting along with others, treating them with
dignity and honor.

With the help of the Holy Spirit and by Your
grace, I will not let any unwholesome talk come out of
my mouth, but only what is helpful for building others
up according to their needs, that it may benefit those
who listen.

My heart overflows with a goodly theme; I address
my psalm to You, the King. My tongue is like the pen of

a ready writer. Mercy and kindness shut out all hatred and selfishness, and truth shuts out all deliberate hypocrisy or falsehood; and I bind them about my neck, write them upon the tablet of my heart.

I speak excellent and princely things; and the opening of my lips shall be for right things. My mouth shall utter truth, and wrongdoing is detestable and loathsome to my lips. All the words of my mouth are righteous (upright and in right standing with You, Lord); there is nothing contrary to truth or crooked in them. My tongue is as choice silver, and my lips feed and guide many. I open my mouth in skillful and godly wisdom, and on my tongue is the law of kindness [giving counsel and instruction].

Father, thank You for loving me unconditionally. I thank You for sending Your Son, Jesus, to be my Friend and elder Brother and for giving me Your Holy Spirit to teach me and to bring all things to my remembrance. I am an overcomer by the blood of the Lamb and by the word of my testimony.

In the name of Jesus I pray, amen.

Scripture References

1 John 3:1

Matthew 6:6

Hebrews 11:6 AMP

Ephesians 5:13 AMP

Proverbs 4:23

Ephesians 4:15

Proverbs 18:21

James 3:5,6 MESSAGE

James 3:9-16 MESSAGE

James 3:17

James 3:17,18 MESSAGE

Ephesians 4:29 NIV

Psalm 45:1 AMP

Proverbs 3:3 AMP

Proverbs 8:6-8 AMP

Proverbs 10:20,21 AMP

Proverbs 31:26 AMP

Romans 8:31-39 NIV

Hebrews 2:11 NIV

John 15:15 NIV

John 14:26

Revelation 12:11

Finding Favor With Others

Father, in the name of Jesus, You make Your face to shine upon and enlighten _____ and are gracious (kind, merciful and giving favor) to him/her. _____ is the head and not the tail. _____ is above only and not beneath.

Thank You for favor for _____ who seeks Your Kingdom and Your righteousness and diligently seeks good. _____ is a blessing to You, Lord, and is a blessing to _____ *(name them: family, neighbors, business associates, etc.).* Grace (favor) is with _____ who loves the Lord Jesus in sincerity. _____ extends favor, honor and love to _____ *(names).* _____ is flowing in Your love, Father. You are pouring out upon _____ the spirit of favor. You crown him/her with glory and honor, for he/she is Your child—Your workmanship.

_____ is a success today. _____ is someone very special with You, Lord. _____ is growing in the Lord—waxing strong in spirit. Father,

You give _____ knowledge and skill in all learning and wisdom.

You bring _____ to find favor, compassion and lovingkindness with _____ *(names)*. _____ obtains favor in the sight of all who look upon him/her this day in the name of Jesus. _____ is filled with Your fullness—rooted and grounded in love. You are doing exceeding abundantly above all that _____ asks or thinks, for Your mighty power is taking over in _____.

Thank You, Father, that _____ is well-favored by You and by man in Jesus' name! Amen.

Scripture References

Numbers 6:25	Psalm 8:5
Deuteronomy 28:13	Ephesians 2:10
Matthew 6:33	Luke 2:40
Proverbs 11:27	Daniel 1:17
Ephesians 6:24	Daniel 1:9
Luke 6:38	Esther 2:15,17
Zechariah 12:10	Ephesians 3:19,20

Single Male Trusting God for a Mate

Father, in the name of Jesus, I believe that You are providing a suitable helpmate for _____. Father, according to Your Word, one who will adapt herself to _____, respect, honor, prefer and esteem him, stand firmly by his side, united in spirit and purpose, having the same love and being in full accord and of one harmonious mind and intention.

Father, You say in Your Word that a wise, understanding and prudent wife is from You, and he who finds a true wife finds a good thing and obtains favor of You.

Father, I know that _____ has found favor in Your sight, and I praise You and thank You for Your Word, knowing that You watch over it to perform it. Amen.

Scripture References

Ephesians 5:22,23	Proverbs 19:14
Proverbs 18:22	Philippians 2:2

Preparing Self for Marriage

Father, sometimes being single can be so lonely, so painful. Seeing people in pairs, laughing and having fun, makes me feel even more alone and different.

Lord, please comfort me in these times. Help me to deal with my feelings and thoughts in an appropriate way. Help me to remember to work hard on myself, so that I will be whole and mature when You bring the right person into my life.

Help me to remember that this is a time of preparation for the day when I will be joined to another human being for life. Show me how to be responsible for myself and how to allow others to be responsible for themselves.

Teach me about boundaries, what they are and how to establish them instead of walls. Teach me about love, Your love, and how to speak the truth in love, as Jesus did.

Father, I don't want to be a hindrance to my future spouse, to You or to myself. Help me to take a good

look at myself, at my self-image. Lead me to people—
teachers, preachers, counselors—and to things—books,
tapes, seminars—anyone and anything You can use to
teach me Your ways of being and doing right and
being whole.

Teach me how to choose the mate You would have
for me. Give me the wisdom I need to see clearly, and
not to be double-minded. Help me to recognize the
qualities You would have me look for in a mate.

Father, thank You for revealing to me that the
choice of a mate is not to be based only on emotions
and feelings, but that You have very definite guidelines
in the Bible for me to use. I know that when I put these
principles into practice, I will save myself a lot of pain
and trouble.

Thank You that You are not trying to make things
hard for me, but that You know me better than I know
myself. You know my situation—You know the beginning from the end. You know the qualities and attributes that are needed in another person that will make
me happy in our shared life together and that person
happy with me.

I pray that You will keep my foot from being caught in a hidden trap or danger. I cast the care of this decision on You, knowing that You will cause my thoughts to come in line with Your will so that my plans will be established and succeed.

In Jesus' name I pray, amen.

Scripture References

1 Corinthians 1:3,4 AMP	James 1:5-8
Ephesians 4:15	Proverbs 3:26 AMP
Matthew 6:33 AMP	Proverbs 16:3 AMP

Husbands

Father, in the beginning You provided a partner for man. Now, I have found a wife to be my partner, and I have obtained favor from the Lord. I will not let mercy and truth forsake me. I bind them around my neck, and write them on the tablet of my heart, and so I find favor and high esteem in the sight of God and man.

In the name of Jesus, I purpose to provide leadership to my wife the way Christ does to His church, not by domineering but by cherishing. I will go all out in my love for her, exactly as Christ did for the church – a love marked by giving, not getting. We are the body of Christ, and when I love my wife, I love myself.

It is my desire to give my wife what is due to her, and I purpose to share my personal rights with her. Father, I am neither anxious nor intimidated, but a good husband to my wife. I honor her, and delight in her. In the new life of God's grace, we are equals. I purpose to treat my wife as an equal so that our prayers will be answered.

LORD, I delight greatly in Your commandments, and my descendants will be mighty on earth, and the generation of the upright will be blessed. Wealth and riches will be in our house, and my righteousness will endure forever.

In the Name of Jesus. Amen

Scripture References

Matthew 18:18	Psalm 112 NKJ
Genesis 2:18 NEB*	Ephesians 5:22-33 MESSAGE
Proverbs 18:22 NKJ	1 Corinthians 7:3-5**
Proverbs 3:3-4 NKJ	1 Peter 3:7-9 MESSAGE
Proverbs 31:28-31 NLB	

---

* *(The Bible from 26 Translations,* © Mathis Publishers, Inc., Moss Point, MS)

** *The New Testament in Modern English,* J. B. Phillips

The Children

Father, in the name of Jesus, I pray and confess Your Word over my children and surround them with my faith—faith in Your Word that You watch over it to perform it! I confess and believe that my children are disciples of Christ taught of the Lord and obedient to Your will. Great is the peace and undisturbed composure of my children, because You, God, contend with that which contends with my children, and You give them safety and ease them.

Father, You will perfect that which concerns me. *I commit and cast the care of my children once and for all over on You, Father.* They are in Your hands, and I am positively persuaded that You are able to guard and keep that which I have committed to You. You are more than enough!

I confess that my children obey their parents in the Lord as His representatives, because this is just and right. My children _____ honor, esteem and value as precious their parents; for this is the first commandment with a promise: that all may be well

with my children and that they may live long on earth. I
believe and confess that my children choose life and love
You, Lord, obey Your voice and cling to You; for You are
their Life and the Length of their days. Therefore, my
children are the head and not the tail, and shall be above
only and not beneath. They are blessed when they come
in and when they go out.

I believe and confess that You give Your angels
charge over my children to accompany and defend and
preserve them in all their ways. You, Lord, are their
Refuge and Fortress. You are their Glory and the Lifter
of their heads.

As parents, we will not provoke, irritate or fret our
children. We will not be hard on them or harass them
or cause them to become discouraged, sullen or morose
or feel inferior and frustrated. We will not break or
wound their spirits, but we will rear them tenderly in
the training, discipline, counsel and admonition of the
Lord. We will train them in the way they should go, and
when they are old they will not depart from it.

O Lord, my Lord, how excellent (majestic and
glorious) is Your name in all the earth! You have set

Your glory on or above the heavens. Out of the mouth of babes and unweaned infants You have established strength because of Your foes, that You might silence the enemy and the avenger. I sing praise to Your name, O Most High. *The enemy is turned back from my children in the name of Jesus!* They increase in wisdom and in favor with God and man. Amen.

Scripture References

Jeremiah 1:12	Psalm 91:11
Isaiah 54:13	Psalm 91:2
Isaiah 49:25	Psalm 3:3
1 Peter 5:7	Colossians 3:21
2 Timothy 1:12	Ephesians 6:4
Ephesians 6:1-3	Proverbs 22:6
Deuteronomy 30:19,20	Psalm 8:1,2
Deuteronomy 28:13	Psalm 9:2,3
Deuteronomy 28:3,6	Luke 2:52

Child's Future

Father, Your Word declares that children are an inheritance from You and promises peace when they are taught in Your ways. I dedicate _____ to You today, that he/she might be raised as You would desire and will follow the path You would choose. Father, I confess Your Word this day over _____. I thank You that Your Word goes out and will not return unto You void, but will accomplish what it says it will do.

Heavenly Father, I commit myself, as a parent, to train _____ in the way he/she should go, trusting in the promise that he/she will not depart from Your ways, but will grow and prosper in them. I turn the care and burden of raising him/her over to You. I will not provoke my child, but will nurture and love him/her in Your care. I will do as the Word of God commands and teach my child diligently. My child will be upon my heart and mind. Your grace is sufficient to overcome my inabilities as a parent.

My child, _____, is obedient and honors both his/her parents, being able to accept the abundant

promises of Your Word of long life and prosperity.
_____ is a godly child; not ashamed or afraid
to honor and keep Your Word. He/she stands convinced
that You are the Almighty God. I am thankful that as
_____ grows, he/she will remember You and
not pass by the opportunity of a relationship with Your
Son, Jesus. Your great blessings will be upon
_____ for keeping Your ways. I thank You
for Your blessings over every area of _____'s
life, that You will see to the salvation and obedience of
his/her life to Your ways.

Heavenly Father, I thank You now that laborers will
be sent into _____'s path, preparing the way
for salvation, as it is written in Your Word, through Your
Son, Jesus. I am thankful that _____ will
recognize the traps of the devil and will be delivered to
salvation through the purity of Your Son. You have
given _____ the grace and the strength to
walk the narrow pathway to Your Kingdom.

I pray that just as Jesus increased in wisdom and
stature, You would bless this child with the same
wisdom and pour out Your favor and wisdom openly to
him/her.

I praise You in advance for _____'s future spouse. Father, Your Word declares that You desire for children to be pure and honorable, waiting upon marriage. I speak blessings to the future union and believe that _____ will be well suited to his/her partner and their household will be in godly order, holding fast to the love of Jesus Christ. Continue to prepare _____ to be the man/woman of God that You desire him/her to be.

_____ shall be diligent and hardworking, never being lazy or undisciplined. Your Word promises great blessing to his/her house, and he/she shall always be satisfied and will always increase. Godliness is profitable unto his/her house, and _____ shall receive the promise of life and all that is to come.

Father, thank You for protecting and guiding my child.

In Jesus' name I pray, amen.

Scripture References

Psalm 127:3   Matthew 7:14

Isaiah 54:13	Luke 2:52
Isaiah 55:11	Hebrews 13:4
Proverbs 22:6	1 Thessalonians 4:3
1 Peter 5:7	Ephesians 5:22-25
Ephesians 6:4	2 Timothy 1:13
Deuteronomy 6:7	Proverbs 13:11
2 Corinthians 12:9	Proverbs 20:13
Ephesians 6:1-3	Romans 12:11
2 Timothy 1:12	1 Timothy 4:8
Proverbs 8:17,32	1 John 3:8
Luke 19:10	John 10:10
Matthew 9:38	Matthew 18:18
2 Corinthians 2:11	John 14:13
2 Timothy 2:26	Psalm 91:1,11
Job 22:30	

Prayer for a Teenager

Father, in the name of Jesus, I affirm Your Word over my son/daughter. I commit _____ to You and delight myself also in You. I thank You that You deliver _____ out of rebellion into right relationship with us, his/her parents.

Father, the first commandment with a promise is to the child who obeys his/her parents in the Lord. You said that all will be well with him/her and he/she will live long on the earth. I affirm this promise on behalf of my child, asking You to give _____ an obedient spirit that he/she may honor (esteem and value as precious) his/her father and mother.

Father, forgive me for mistakes made out of my own unresolved hurts or selfishness which may have caused _____ hurt. I release the anointing that is upon Jesus to bind up and heal our (parents' and child's) broken hearts. Give us the ability to understand and forgive one another as God for Christ's sake has forgiven us. Thank You for the Holy Spirit Who leads us into all truth and corrects erroneous perceptions about past or present situations.

Thank You for teaching us to listen to each other and giving _____ an ear that hears admonition, for then he/she will be called wise. I affirm that I will speak excellent and princely things and the opening of my lips shall be for right things. Father, I commit to train and teach _____ in the way that he/she is to go and when _____ is old he/she will not depart from sound doctrine and teaching, but will follow it all the days of his/her life. In the name of Jesus, I command rebellion to be far from the heart of my child and confess that he/she is willing and obedient, free to enjoy the reward of Your promises. _____ shall be peaceful, bringing peace to others.

Father, according to Your Word we have been given the ministry of reconciliation and I release this ministry and the word of reconciliation into this family situation. I refuse to provoke or irritate or fret my child, I will not be hard on him/her lest he/she becomes discouraged, feeling inferior and frustrated. I will not break his/her spirit, in the name of Jesus and by the power of the Holy Spirit. Father, I forgive my child for the wrongs which he/she has done and thank You that he/she comes to his/her senses and escapes out of the snare of the enemy (rebellion). Thank You for watching over Your Word to perform it, turning and reconciling the heart of the child to the parents and the hearts of the parents to the child. Thank You for bringing my child into a healthy relationship with You and with me that our lives might glorify You! Amen.

Scripture References

Psalm 55:12-14	Proverbs 8:6,7
1 Peter 5:7	Proverbs 22:6
Psalm 37:4	Isaiah 1:19
John 14:6	Isaiah 54:13
Ephesians 6:1-3	2 Corinthians 5:18,19
1 John 1:9	Colossians 3:21
Isaiah 61:1	John 20:23
John 16:13	Ezekiel 22:30
Proverbs 15:31	Jeremiah 1:12
Proverbs 13:1	Malachi 4:6

Children at School

Father, in Jesus' name, I confess Your Word this day concerning my children as they pursue their education and training at school. You are effectually at work in them creating within them the power and desire to please You. They are the head and not the tail, above and not beneath.

I pray that my children will find favor, good understanding and high esteem in the sight of God and their teachers and classmates. I ask You to give my children wisdom and understanding as knowledge is presented to them in all fields of study and endeavor.

Father, thank You for giving my children an appreciation for education and helping them to understand that the Source and beginning of all knowledge is You. They have the appetite of the diligent, and they are abundantly supplied with educational resources; and their thoughts are those of the steadily diligent, which tend only to achievement. Thank You that they are growing in wisdom and knowledge. I will not cease to

pray for them, asking that they be filled with the knowledge of Your will, bearing fruit in every good work.

Father, I thank You that my children have divine protection since they dwell in the secret place of the Most High. My children trust and find their refuge in You and stand rooted and grounded in Your love. They shall not be led astray by philosophies of men and teaching that is contrary to truth. You are their Shield and Buckler, protecting them from attacks or threats. Thank You for the angels which You have assigned to them to accompany, defend and preserve them in all their ways of obedience and service. My children are established in You love, which drives all fear out of doors.

I pray that the teachers of my children will be godly men and women of integrity. Give our teachers understanding hearts and wisdom in order that they may walk in the ways of piety and virtue, revering Your holy name. Amen.

Scripture References

Philippians 2:13   Psalm 91:1,2

Deuteronomy 28:1,2,13   Ephesians 4:14

Proverbs 3:4

1 Kings 4:29

Daniel 1:4

Proverbs 1:4,7

Proverbs 3:13

Proverbs 4:5

Colossians 1:9,10

Psalm 91:3-11

Ephesians 1:17

Psalm 112:8

Ephesians 3:17

Matthew 18:18

James 1:5

The Home

Father, I thank You that You have blessed me with all spiritual blessings in Christ Jesus.

Through skillful and godly wisdom is my house (my life, my home, my family) built, and by understanding it is established on a sound and good foundation. And by knowledge shall the chambers (of its every area) be filled with all precious and pleasant riches—great priceless treasure. The house of the uncompromisingly righteous shall stand. Prosperity and welfare are in my house in the name of Jesus.

My house is securely built. It is founded on a rock—revelation knowledge of Your Word, Father. Jesus is my Cornerstone. Jesus is Lord of my household. Jesus is our Lord—spirit, soul and body.

Whatever may be our task, we work at it heartily as something done for You, Lord, and not for men. We love each other with the God kind of love, and we dwell in peace. My home is deposited into Your charge, entrusted to Your protection and care.

Father, as for me and my house we shall serve the Lord in Jesus' name. Hallelujah! Amen.

Scripture References

Ephesians 1:3

Proverbs 24:3,4 AMP

Proverbs 15:6

Proverbs 12:7 AMP

Psalm 112:3

Luke 6:48

Acts 4:11

Acts 16:31

Philippians 2:10,11

Colossians 3:23

Colossians 3:14,15

Acts 20:32

Joshua 24:15

Complete in Him as a Single

Father, we thank You that _____ desires and earnestly seeks first after the things of Your Kingdom. We thank You that he/she knows that You love him/her and that he/she can trust Your Word.

For in Jesus the whole fullness of Deity (the Godhead) continues to dwell in bodily form—giving complete expression of the Divine Nature, and _____ is in Him and has come to the fullness of life in Christ. He/she is filled with the Godhead— Father, Son and Holy Spirit—and he/she reaches full spiritual stature. And Christ is the Head of all rule and authority—of every angelic principality and power.

So because of Jesus, _____ is complete; Jesus is his/her Lord. He/she comes before You, Father, desiring a born-again Christian mate. We petition that Your will be done in his/her life. Now we enter into that blessed rest by adhering to, trusting in and relying on You, in the name of Jesus. Amen.

Scripture References

Colossians 2:9,10 AMP   Hebrews 4:10 AMP

Part 3

PRAYERS FOR CAREER

Beginning Each Day

Father, as the _____ *(owner, president, chair-man, manager, supervisor)* of _____ *(name of company),* I come before You rejoicing, for this is the day which You have made and I will be glad in it. To obey is better than sacrifice, so I am making a decision to submit to Your will today that my plans and purposes may be conducted in a manner that will bring honor and glory to You. Cause me to be spiritually and mentally alert in this time of meditation and prayer.

It is into Your keeping that I place my family—my parents, spouse, children and grandchildren—knowing that You are able to keep that which I commit to You against that Day. Thank You for the angels that You have commanded concerning me and my family to guard us in all our ways; they will lift us up in their hands so that we will not strike our foot against a stone.

Thank You, Lord, for the tremendous success that my associates and I have experienced in our organization and for the increase in profits and productivity we have enjoyed. Thank You for continuing to influence every person in this business and every decision that is made. Thank You for Your faithfulness to us day by day and for helping us to become all that You desire us to be.

Thank You, Father, for helping to make us a company that continues to grow and expand. We recognize that without Your help, it would not be possible. Without Your direction and guidance, we would be failures; with it we can prosper and have good success. I continue to thank You for the many blessings that You have poured out upon us all.

I especially thank You for the co-laborers with whom I will be interacting today. Give me words of wisdom, words of grace, that I might encourage them and build them up.

Father, I kneel before You, from Whom Your whole family in heaven and on earth derives its name. I pray that out of Your glorious riches You may strengthen each one with power through Your Spirit in his inner being, so that Christ may dwell in each heart through faith.

Now to Him Who is able to do immeasurably more than all we ask or imagine, according to His power that is at work within us, to Him be the glory in this company and in Christ Jesus throughout all generations, for ever and ever! In Jesus' name I pray. Amen.

Scripture References

Psalm 118:24	Lamentations 3:22,23
1 Samuel 15:22	Joshua 1:8
2 Timothy 1:12	Ephesians 3:14-17 NIV
Psalm 91:11,12 NIV	Ephesians 3:20 NIV

Being Equipped for Success

Father, I thank You that the entrance of Your words gives light. I thank You that Your Word which You speak *(and which I speak)* is alive and full of power [making it active, operative, energizing and effective].

I thank You, Father, that [You have given me a spirit] of power and of love and of a calm and well-balanced mind and discipline and self-control. I have Your power and ability and sufficiency, for You have qualified me [making me to be fit and worthy and sufficient] as a minister and dispenser of a new covenant [of salvation through Christ].

In the name of Jesus, I walk out of the realm of failure into the arena of success, giving thanks to You, Father, for You have qualified and made me fit to share the portion which is the inheritance of the saints (Your holy people) in the Light.

Father, You have delivered and drawn me to Yourself out of the control and dominion of darkness *(failure, doubt and fear)* and have transferred me into the Kingdom of the Son of Your love.

I praise God, the Father of my Lord Jesus Christ,
Who has blessed me with every blessing in heaven
because I belong to Christ. Your divine power has given
me everything I need for life and godliness through my
knowledge of Him Who called me by His own glory
and goodness. I rejoice in Jesus Who has come that I
might have life and have it more abundantly.

I am a new creation, for I am (engrafted) in Christ,
the Messiah. The old [previous moral and spiritual
condition] has passed away. Behold, the fresh and new
has come! I forget those things which are behind me
and reach forth unto those things which are before me. I
am crucified with Christ: nevertheless I live; yet not I,
but Christ lives in me: and the life which I now live in
the flesh I live by the faith of the Son of God, Who
loved me and gave Himself for me.

Father, I attend to Your Word. I consent and
submit to Your sayings. Your words shall not depart
from my sight; I will keep them in the center of my
heart. For they are life *(success)* to me, healing and health
to all my flesh. I keep and guard my heart with all vigi-
lance; and above all, that I guard, for out of it flows the
springs of life.

I will not let mercy and kindness and truth forsake me. I bind them about my neck; I write them upon the tablet of my heart. So therefore I will find favor, good understanding and high esteem in the sight [or judgment] of God and man.

Father, my delight and desire are in Your Law, and on it I habitually meditate (ponder and study) by day and by night. Therefore I am like a tree firmly planted [and tended] by the streams of water, ready to bring forth my fruit in my season; my leaf also shall not fade or wither, and everything I do shall prosper [and come to maturity].

Now thanks be unto God, which always causeth us to triumph in Christ!

In Jesus' name I pray, amen.

Scripture References

Psalm 119:130	2 Corinthians 5:17 AMP
Hebrews 4:12 AMP	Philippians 3:13
2 Timothy 1:7 AMP	Galatians 2:20
2 Corinthians 3:5 AMP	Proverbs 4:20-23 AMP

Colossians 1:12,13 AMP   Proverbs 3:3,4 AMP

Ephesians 1:3 TLB   Psalm 1:2,3 AMP

2 Peter 1:3 NIV   2 Corinthians 2:14

John 10:10 AMP

Assuring the Success of a Business

Father, I come before You with thanksgiving. You have qualified and made me fit to share the portion which is the inheritance of the saints (Your holy people) in the light. You have delivered me out of the power of darkness and translated me into the Kingdom of Your dear Son.

As I know You better, You will give me, through Your great power, everything I need for living a truly good life: You even share Your own glory and Your own goodness with me! And by that same mighty power You have given me all the other rich and wonderful blessings You promised; for instance, the promise to save me from the lust and rottenness all around me and to give me Your own character.

You have delivered me out of the power of darkness and translated me into the Kingdom of Your dear Son.

Where Your Word is, there is light and understanding. Your Word does not return to You void, but it always accomplishes what it is sent to do.

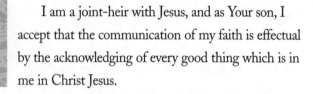
I am a joint-heir with Jesus, and as Your son, I accept that the communication of my faith is effectual by the acknowledging of every good thing which is in me in Christ Jesus.

Father, I commit my works (the plans and cares of my business) to You, trusting them wholly to You. Since You are effectually at work in me [You cause my thoughts to become agreeable with Your will] so that my (business) plans shall be established and succeed.

In the name of Jesus, I submit to every kind of wisdom and understanding (practical insight and prudence) which You have lavished upon me in accordance with the riches and generosity of Your gracious favor.

Father, I affirm that I obey Your Word by making an honest living with my own hands so that I may be able to give to those in need. In Your strength and according to Your grace, I provide for myself and my own family.

Thank You, Father, for making all grace (every favor and earthly blessing) come to me in abundance, so that I, having all sufficiency in all things, may abound to every good work.

Father, thank You for the ministering spirits that You have assigned to go forth to minister on my behalf and bring in trade. Jesus said that those who put their faith and trust in Him are the light of the world. In His name my light shall so shine before all men that they may see my good works and glorify You, my Heavenly Father.

Thank You for the grace to remain diligent in seeking knowledge and skill in areas in which I am inexperienced. I ask You for wisdom and the ability to understand righteousness, justice and fair dealing [in every area and relationship]. I affirm that I am faithful and committed to Your Word. My life and business are founded upon its principles.

Thank You, Father, for the success of my business!

In Jesus' name I pray, amen.

Scripture References

Colossians 1:12 AMP   Ephesians 4:28 AMP

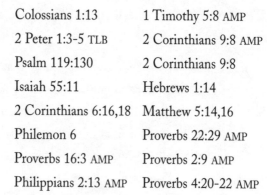

Colossians 1:13

2 Peter 1:3-5 TLB

Psalm 119:130

Isaiah 55:11

2 Corinthians 6:16,18

Philemon 6

Proverbs 16:3 AMP

Philippians 2:13 AMP

Ephesians 1:7,8 AMP

1 Timothy 5:8 AMP

2 Corinthians 9:8 AMP

2 Corinthians 9:8

Hebrews 1:14

Matthew 5:14,16

Proverbs 22:29 AMP

Proverbs 2:9 AMP

Proverbs 4:20-22 AMP

Making a Difficult Decision

Father, I bring this decision before You. It is a difficult one for me to make in the natural, but I know that with You it can be an easy one.

I ask You, Lord, to help me see both sides of this issue and to consider all the facts involved in it. Help me to properly evaluate both the positive and negative attributes of this situation.

Lord, I recognize that an important part of being an excellent manager is decisiveness. In processing the information and considering the possible repercussions or benefits of this decision, help me to avoid the paralysis of analysis. Help me to get the information I need and to evaluate it carefully and wisely.

Help me, Father, to hear Your voice, and so to make the right and correct decision in this case. Keep me from acting in haste but also from delaying too long to reach a decision.

Father, help me not to be influenced by my own personal wants or desires concerning this matter under

consideration. Instead help me to perceive and choose
what is best for my department or company, regardless
of how I may feel about it personally. Help me to
undertake and carry out this decision-making process
accurately and objectively.

Thank You for Your guidance and direction in
this situation.

In Jesus' name I pray, amen.

Scripture References

Isaiah 11:2 AMP	John 10:27
Colossians 4:1 NIV	Philippians 2:3 NIV
Proverbs 28:1	Judges 6:12

Prayer for the Company

Father, I pray for _____ today. I thank You for this organization and for the opportunity to be a part of it. I am grateful for the chance to earn the income this firm provides for me and my family and for the blessing that it has been to me and all its employees.

Father, I thank You that_____ enjoys a good reputation, that it is seen well in the minds of its customers and vendors. Thank You that it prospers and makes a profit, that You give it favor with its clients, that You continue to provide wisdom and insight to those within it who occupy important decision-making positions.

It is my prayer that _____ will continue to thrive and prosper. Thank You for increased sales and expanded markets.

Thank You, Father, for the creativity that is evident in the different areas of the company—new product ideas and new servicing concepts—innovations and techniques that keep this organization vibrant, alive and thriving.

I ask You, Lord, to bless it and to cause it to be a blessing to the market it serves, as well as to all those whose lives are invested in it on a daily basis.

In Jesus' name I pray, amen.

Scripture References

1 Timothy 2:1-3	Proverbs 3:21
3 John 2	Psalm 115:14
Joshua 1:8	Proverbs 8:12
Psalm 5:12	Malachi 3:12 AMP
Proverbs 2:7	Hebrews 6:14

Prayer for a Superior

Father, in Your Word, You said to pray for those who exercise authority over us, so I pray for my manager/supervisor today. I ask You to give him/her clarity of thought concerning every decision made this day. Help him/her to clearly identify and accurately assess every potential problem. Help him/her to make the right decisions—to respond, and not to react, to whatever situation or circumstance might arise during the course of the day.

I ask You, Father, to help him/her to set the proper priorities today. Reveal to him/her what tasks are most important and cause him/her to inspire us to perform our duties to the best of our abilities.

I ask that You help him/her to be sensitive to the needs of those under his/her supervision, those who work for him/her. Help him/her to realize that not everyone is the same and that no two people respond or react in the same way. Help him/her to adapt his/her management style or technique to the strengths, weaknesses and personality type of each

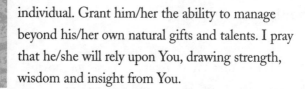
individual. Grant him/her the ability to manage
beyond his/her own natural gifts and talents. I pray
that he/she will rely upon You, drawing strength,
wisdom and insight from You.

I purpose in my heart to set a guard over my
mouth. I refuse to say anything negative or disrespectful
about my manager/supervisor. I choose to support
him/her and to say only good things about him/her.

Lord, I ask You to give him/her a peaceful spirit, so
that even in the midst of great turmoil he/she may act
with surety and confidence and make wise decisions.
Help me to be sensitive to his/her needs and responsibilities. Show me ways, Lord, to support him/her and to
assist him/her in the performance of his/her duties.

Father, You have said in Your Word that Your Spirit
will show us things to come. I ask You to show my
manager/supervisor the solution to small problems
before they become major problems. Grant him/her
creative ideas on how he/she can better lead and manage
his/her department.

For all these things I give You thanks, praise and
glory, in Jesus' name. Amen.

Scripture References

1 Timothy 2:1-3 AMP   Isaiah 40:29-31 AMP

1 Corinthians 2:16   Philippians 4:7

Ephesians 4:23,24   Hebrews 12:14

Matthew 6:33 AMP   John 14:26

Romans 12:10   John 16:13

Prayer When Persecuted at Work

Father, I come to You in the name that is above all other names—the name of Jesus. Your name is a strong tower that I can run into and be safe when I am persecuted on the job.

Lord, I admit that these unkind words really hurt me. I desire to be accepted by my boss and co-workers, but I long to obey You and follow Your commandments. I know that Jesus was tempted just as I am, but He didn't give in to sin or hate. Please give me Your mercy and grace to deal with this situation. I look to You for my comfort; You are a true friend at all times.

Thank You, Lord, for never leaving me alone or rejecting me. I make a decision to forgive the people who have spoken unkind words about me. I ask You to work this forgiveness in my heart. I submit to You and reject the disappointment and anger that have attempted to consume me. Specifically, right now I forgive _____.

I ask You to cause this situation to accommodate itself for good in my life. **To you, O Lord, I lift up my** soul; in you I trust, O my God. Do not let me be put to shame, nor let my enemies triumph over me (Ps. 25:1,2 NIV). Because I love You, O Lord, You will rescue me; You will protect me because I acknowledge Your name. I will call upon You, and You will deliver me. You will be with me in trouble; You will deliver me and honor me.

Father, I resist the temptation to strike back in anger. I purpose to love _____ with the love of Jesus in me. Mercy and truth are written upon the tablets of my heart; therefore, You will cause me to find favor and understanding with my boss and co-workers. Keep me from self-righteousness so that I may walk in Your righteousness. Thank You for sending and giving me friends who will stand by me and teach me how to guard my heart with all diligence.

I declare that in the midst of all these things I am more than a conqueror through Jesus Who loves me, and I will be confident in Your wisdom when working. I am of good courage and pray that freedom of utterance be given to me as I do my job.

In Jesus' name I pray, amen.

Scripture References

Philippians 2:9

Proverbs 18:10

Hebrews 4:15

Proverbs 17:17

Hebrews 13:5

Proverbs 16:4 AMP

Psalm 91:14,15 NIV

Proverbs 3:3,4

Proverbs 4:23

Romans 8:37

Proverbs 8:12

Psalm 31:24

Ephesians 6:19

Office Staff

Introduction

Our prayer coordinator wrote this prayer for our ministry. It may be used for the members of any ministry or outreach that depends upon the Holy Spirit to go before it and prepare the way for its labor with and for the Lord.

Prayer

Father, we begin this day rejoicing in You. We thank You for Your goodness, mercy and grace toward us as individuals and as a ministry. We confess and proclaim that this is the day that You have made, and we purpose to rejoice and be glad in it.

Father, we lift up the day with its activities, its relationships, its decisions and creativity. We offer it all up to You, acknowledging Jesus as Lord of all and asking You by Your Holy Spirit to use it for Your glory and honor. We pray for Your will to be done in us individually and as a ministry.

We plead the blood of Jesus over this property, all staff members, every telephone contact, every person who enters these doors and the entire ministry network, including all those for whom we pray. We thank You for delivering us from the authority of darkness and translating us into the Kingdom of Your dear Son. We are living and growing up in the Kingdom of light.

Father, You have given us choices. We choose life and blessings. You are our Strength, our Confidence and our Courage. We are courageous, boldly proclaiming that Your anointing—Your burden-removing, yoke-destroying power—is abiding in us individually and collectively. This anointing is working in, on and through us this day to accomplish Your will. May You be glorified in all that we do.

Thank You for Your love. We are imitators of You—walking in love, in truth, in light and in wisdom inside and outside these offices. We are well-balanced and enduring in all things.

We are asking for and expecting the former and latter rains to be poured out on this ministry to fulfill Your assignments. You have called us by Your grace for

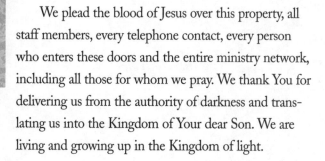

such a time as this. We rejoice in the outpouring of Your Spirit on this ministry.

In the name of Jesus, amen.

Scripture References

Psalm 33:1	1 John 2:27
Psalm 118:24	1 Corinthians 6:20
1 Corinthians 12:3	Ephesians 5:1,2 AMP
Matthew 6:10	James 5:7
Colossians 1:13	1 Peter 5:10
Deuteronomy 30:19	Esther 4:14
Isaiah 10:27	Acts 2:17

Improving Harmony and Cooperation

Devotional Reading

**Fill up and complete my joy by living in
harmony and being of the same mind and
one in purpose, having the same love, being
in full accord and of one harmonious mind
and intention.**

Philippians 2:2 AMP

Prayer

Father, Jesus prayed that His followers would be
one. I enter into agreement with my Lord, praying for
the development of harmony and cooperation among the
leadership and employees of _____ *(company
name)*. I ask for wisdom to know how to resolve any
conflicts that may have arisen among the departments.

As _____ *(president, supervisor, manager, etc.)*
of _____ I institute the principles of peace,
uprooting and dissolving confusion, rivalries, arguments

and disagreements for the good of our company,
_____, and the welfare of all concerned.

In the name of Jesus I submit myself to You,
Father, and resist the devil. I overcome the fear of
confrontation (and its outcome) and initiate resolution. I
desire to pursue peace with my co-workers, customers,
family and friends.

Give me the courage to go to anyone who is
holding anything against me that we might be reconciled. Then I will come and offer my gift to You.

Also, I ask for the boldness of the Lion of Judah to
go to anyone who has sinned against me and _____
(company name), confronting his/her fault without
attacking him/her. I am requesting and believing for
reconciliation. Help me to forgive even if he/she refuses
to be reconciled and follow through with the necessary
steps for his/her good and the company's welfare.

Thank You for the harmony and cooperation
necessary to accomplish our common goals.

Glory be to You Who by Your mighty power at
work within us is able to do far more than we would
ever dare to ask or even dream of—infinitely beyond our

highest prayers, desires, thoughts or hopes. May You be given glory forever and ever through endless ages because of Your master plan of salvation for the church through Jesus Christ.

In Jesus' name I pray, amen.

Scripture References

John 17:21

James 1:5

James 4:7

Hebrews 12:14 NKJV

Matthew 5:23,24

Matthew 18:15

Ephesians 3:20,21 TLB

Overcoming Negative Work Attitudes

Thank You, Father, for watching over Your Word to perform it as I speak it over myself and those who work with me in Your service, especially
_____. I say that he/she is obedient to his/her employers—bosses or supervisors—having respect for them and being eager to please them, in singleness of motive and with all his/her heart, as [service] to Christ [Himself]. Not in the way of eye-service [as if they were watching him/her] but as a servant (employee) of Christ, doing Your will heartily and with his/her whole soul.

_____ readily renders service with goodwill, as to You and not to men. He/she knows that for whatever good he/she does, he/she will receive his/her reward from You.

_____ does all things without grumbling and faultfinding and complaining [against You] and questioning and doubting [within himself/herself]. He/she is blameless and guileless, Your child, without blemish (faultless, unrebukable) in the midst of a crooked and wicked generation [spiritually perverted and perverse], among whom he/she is seen as a bright light (a star or beacon shining out clearly) in the [dark] world.

_____ reveres You, Lord, and his/her work is a sincere expression of his/her devotion to You. Whatever may be his/her task, he/she works at it heartily (from the soul), as something done for You, knowing that [The One Whom] he/she is actually serving [is] the Lord Christ (the Messiah).

In His name I pray, amen.

Scripture References (AMP)

Jeremiah 12:1	Philippians 2:14,15
Ephesians 6:5-8	Colossians 3:22-24

Prayer for an Increase in Personal Productivity

Father, I come to You out of frustration because I am not pleased with my performance on the job. It seems that I am not producing that which I should be producing because I am just not as efficient or effective as I need to be.

Lord, I ask for Your help in planning my day, paying attention to my duties, staying focused on my assignment, establishing priorities in my work and making steady progress toward my objectives.

Give me insight, Father. Help me to see any habits that I may have that might tend to make me nonproductive. Reveal to me ways to better handle the tedious tasks I must perform so that I can achieve the greatest results possible. Help me to organize my efforts, schedule my activities and budget my time.

From books, by Your Spirit, through the people who work with me or by whatever means You choose, Lord, reveal to me that which I need to know and do in order to become a more productive, fruitful worker.

My heart's desire is to give my very best to You and to my employer. When I become frustrated because that is not taking place, help me, Father, by the power of Your Spirit to do whatever is necessary to correct that situation so that I can once again function with accuracy and proficiency.

Thank You, Lord, for bringing all these things to pass in my life.

In Jesus' name I pray, amen.

Scripture References

Psalm 118:24	Psalm 119:99 AMP
Proverbs 16:9 AMP	Proverbs 9:10 AMP
Proverbs 19:21 AMP	1 Corinthians 4:5
Ephesians 1:17	

Conducting a Meeting

Father, in the name of Jesus, may Your wisdom prevail today in our meeting. Help each of us to be quick to listen, slow to speak and slow to become angry, for man's anger does not bring about the righteous life that You desire.

Lord, I recognize Your Holy Spirit and welcome Him to the meeting, acknowledging our dependence upon His presence and guidance. With His help, I purpose to respect and regard every individual's opinions as valuable and worthy of consideration. Knowing that a soft answer turns away wrath, I will be polite and courteous in all our deliberations.

Help each one of us to offer our opinions at the appropriate time and to resist any feelings of self-pity or self-aggrandizement. Guard us from thinking that our opinions are not being heard.

I pray for those who have to deal with rejection. Help them to know that any negation of their opinions or suggestions is not personal.

Should my own opinions be rejected, I refuse to believe that I, personally, am rejected. I will remember that my opinions are not me.

Father, Your love in me does not insist on its own rights or its own way, for it is not self-seeking. I submit to the wisdom that comes from heaven for it is pure, peace loving, considerate, full of mercy and good fruit, impartial and sincere. As a peacemaker, I sow in peace, reaping a harvest of righteousness.

Thank You, Father, for wisdom that is from above.

In Jesus' name I pray, amen.

Scripture References

Ephesians 1:17	1 Peter 5:5 NIV
James 1:19,20 NIV	Romans 12:10 NIV
John 16:13	1 Corinthians 13:5 AMP
Proverbs 15:1	James 3:17,18 NIV

Facing a Financial Crisis

Lord, I come to You in this time of great need in the life of our organization. Whatever the cause, we find ourselves in extreme financial need.

First of all, Father, I come against the spirit of fear in the name of Jesus. I refuse to operate in fear, anxiety or worry concerning this situation. I know it is serious, and I do not approach it flippantly. But, I know that if there is fear, anxiety or worry in my heart, it will cloud my judgment and appraisal of the situation. It will make it seem even worse than it really is. It will also block my ability to hear from You.

Father, I give this whole situation to You and ask for Your guidance and direction in rectifying it. If it came about because of any bad decisions I made or any wrong thoughts or actions I engaged in, I repent to You right now. I ask You for forgiveness. Help me to see my mistakes and faults and to do all in my power to overcome and correct them.

Lord, if this financial crisis is the result of my negligence or my irresponsible spending, I ask You to forgive

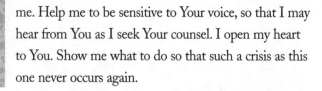

me. Help me to be sensitive to Your voice, so that I may hear from You as I seek Your counsel. I open my heart to You. Show me what to do so that such a crisis as this one never occurs again.

Concerning the current need, I ask You to help me in this present crisis. Give me favor with those to whom we owe money. I thank You for an increase in sales so that our income can grow, knowledge so we will know where to cut expenses and insight so we will know how to budget the money that we do have.

Thank You for supernatural wisdom so we can see how to walk out of this terrible situation. Help us to formulate a plan of recovery, a plan to get from where we are today to where we want to be tomorrow. Help me to communicate that plan clearly and effectively to the ones who will be involved in it.

Lord, send me counselors, those who can help me with this task. Send me people with wisdom and insight concerning this situation that they might help me perceive and discern Your perfect plan for recovery.

Father, I give myself entirely to You. Thank You that I hear Your voice accurately and distinctly as You reveal to me what to do and how to do it. I ask You to help me identify the reason why we got into this crisis in the first place and to erect safeguards so that it will never happen again.

Thank You for Your forgiveness, Your help, Your wisdom and Your instruction. Thank You that we are totally and completely out of this crisis. I receive it by faith and thank You that it is done, in Jesus' name. Amen.

Scripture References

2 Timothy 1:7	Acts 6:10
Philippians 4:6 AMP	Psalm 1:1
Ephesians 5:17	Psalm 16:7 AMP
John 10:27 NIV	Psalm 73:24
Psalm 5:12	Proverbs 15:22 NIV
Psalm 115:14	Job 22:28
Daniel 2:21-23 AMP	

To Honor God in Business Dealings

Father, You are love, and I desire to be an imitator of You that Your life may be manifested this day to my employees.

Thank You for wise counsel, for giving me ears to hear and for helping me to analyze all that I say and do for the good and betterment of my staff. Help me to speak truly, deal truly and live truly in harmony with You, myself and my co-laborers. In all my ways I acknowledge You, and You direct my ways.

Because I commit to You the decisions that I am responsible for making, You cause my thoughts to become agreeable to Your will and so my plans shall be established and succeed. Thank You for the courage to say no when it is necessary for the good of this company and in keeping with Your plan and purpose for it.

We are an interdependent people—mutually dependent one upon the other. Each department operates in harmony and agreement—not [merely] concerned with its own interests, but also with the interests of others.

As an example to my employees, I commit to do to others what I would have them do to me. It is my desire to walk uprightly before You; therefore, I consider, direct and establish my way with the confidence of integrity.

You are my confidence, and it is You Who keep my foot from being snared. Your love is shed abroad in my heart so that I love my neighbor as myself.

In Jesus' name I pray, amen.

Scripture References

1 John 4:8	Philippians 2:4 AMP
Ephesians 5:1 NIV	Matthew 7:12 NIV
Ephesians 4:15 AMP	Proverbs 3:26 NIV
Proverbs 3:6	Romans 5:5
Proverbs 16:3 AMP	

Analyzing a Report

Lord, I come to You in prayer before I begin to analyze this report before me. I recognize that this is information I need in order to function properly and to fulfill my responsibilities.

I ask You, Father, to help me to analyze this report accurately and to draw from it what I need to make wise decisions.

Show me, Lord, not only those things that are obvious, but also those that are not readily apparent to the natural human eye. Increase my understanding. If there is more information needed, help me to determine what it is and how to go about getting it.

Help me to be able to assimilate vital data and facts and to reduce them to their bare essentials. Give me discernment to notice any trends, either positive or negative, that are developing within my department and/or company. Help me to take the information and knowledge I gain and use it to better carry out my duties.

Help me to take what You are showing me and apply it to my daily activities so that I may enhance my overall job performance and improve the success rate of my department and this organization.

In Jesus' name I pray, amen.

Scripture References

Matthew 7:7,8 NIV	Proverbs 2:11 NIV
Ephesians 1:17	Daniel 11:32 AMP
Ephesians 3:20 AMP	Joshua 1:8 NIV
Proverbs 4:11 AMP	Mathew 6:33

Part Four
PRAYERS FOR MINISTRY

The Body of Christ

Father, You put all things under the feet of Jesus and gave Him to be head over all things to the church which is His body, the fullness of Him who fills all in all. We were dead in trespasses and sins, but You made us alive! Christ is our peace, and we are no longer strangers and foreigners, but fellow citizens with the saints and members of the household of God. Jesus is our Cornerstone.

Father, You want us to grow up, to know the whole truth and tell it in love – like Christ in everything. We take our lead from Christ, Who is the source of everything we do. He keeps us in step with each other. His very breath and blood flow through us, nourishing us so that we will grow up healthy in God, robust in love.

May we be filled with the knowledge of Your will in all wisdom and spiritual understanding. As the elect of God, holy and beloved, we put on tender mercies, kindness, humility, meekness, longsuffering; bearing with one another, and forgiving one another. If we have a complaint against another; even as Christ forgave us,

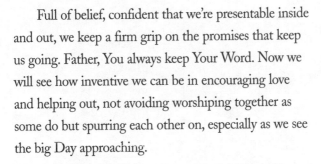

so we also must do. Above all things, we put on love, which is the bond of perfection, and let the peace of God rule in our hearts, to which also we were called in one body, and we are thankful.

Full of belief, confident that we're presentable inside and out, we keep a firm grip on the promises that keep us going. Father, You always keep Your Word. Now we will see how inventive we can be in encouraging love and helping out, not avoiding worshiping together as some do but spurring each other on, especially as we see the big Day approaching.

Since we are all called to travel on the same road and in the same direction, we will stay together, both outwardly and inwardly. We have one Master, one faith, one baptism, one God and Father of all, Who rules over all, works through all, and is present in all. Everything we are and think and do is permeated with oneness.

Father, we commit to pray for one another, keeping our eyes open, and keeping each other's spirits up so that no one falls behind or drops out. Also, we pray for our spiritual leaders that they will know what to say and have the courage to say it at the right time.

We are one in the bonds of love, in the name of Jesus.

Scripture References

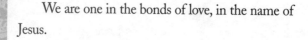

Ephesians 1:22-23 NKJ   Colossians 3:12-15 NKJ

Ephesians 4:15-16   Ephesians 4:4-6
  MESSAGE   MESSAGE

Hebrew 10:23-25   Ephesians 6:18-19
  MESSAGE   MESSAGE

Salvation of the Lost

Father, it is written in Your Word, **First of all, then, I admonish and urge that petitions, prayers, intercessions and thanksgivings be offered on behalf of all men** (1 Timothy 2:1 AMP).

Therefore, Father, we bring the lost of the world this day—every man, woman and child from here to the farthest corner of the earth—before You. As we intercede, we use our faith, believing that thousands this day have the opportunity to make Jesus their Lord.

Father, we know that Satan would prevent these from hearing truth, if possible. We are human, but we don't wage war with human plans and methods. We use God's mighty weapons, to knock down the devil's strongholds. With these weapons we break down every proud argument that keeps people from knowing God. With these weapons we conquer their rebellious ideas, and teach them to obey Christ.

We ask the Lord of the harvest to thrust the perfect laborers across these lives this day to share the good news of the Gospel in a special way so that they will listen and understand it. We believe that they will not be able to resist the wooing of the Holy Spirit, for you, Father, bring them to repentance by Your goodness and love.

We confess that they shall see who have never been told of Jesus. They shall understand who have never heard of Jesus. And they shall come out of the snare of the devil who has held them captive. They shall open their eyes and turn from darkness to light—from the power of Satan to You, God!

In Jesus' name, amen.

Scripture References

1 Timothy 2:1,2 AMP Romans 2:4

2 Corinthians 10:35 NLT Romans 15:21 AMP

Matthew 9:38   2 Timothy 2:26 AMP

Matthew 18:18

Vision for a Church

Father, in the name of Jesus, we come into Your
presence thanking You for _____(name of
church). You have called us to be saints in

_____(name of city) and around the world.
As we lift our voices in one accord, we recognize that
You are God, and everything was made by and for You.
We call into being those things that be not as though
they were.

We thank You that we all speak the same thing:
There is no division among us; we are perfectly joined
together in the same mind. Grant unto us, Your representatives here, a boldness to speak Your Word which
You will confirm with signs following. We thank You
that we have workmen in abundance and all manner of
cunning people for every manner of work. Each department operates in the excellence of ministry and intercession. We have in our church the ministry gifts for the
edifying of this body till we all come into the unity of
the faith and the knowledge of the Son of God, unto a

mature person. None of our people will be children, tossed to and fro and carried about with every wind of doctrine. We speak the truth in love.

We are a growing and witnessing body of believers becoming _____ (number) strong. We have every need met. Therefore, we meet the needs of people who come—spirit, soul and body. We ask for the wisdom of God in meeting these needs. Father, we thank You for the ministry facilities that will more than meet the needs of the ministry You have called us to. Our church is prospering financially, and we have more than enough to meet every situation. We have everything we need to carry out Your Great Commission and reach the _____ (name of city or country) area for Jesus. We are a people of love as love is shed abroad in our hearts by the Holy Spirit. We thank You that the Word of God is living big in all of us, and Jesus is Lord!

We are a supernatural church, composed of supernatural people doing supernatural things, for we are laborers together with God. We thank You for Your

presence among us, and we lift our hands and praise
Your holy name! Amen.

Scripture References

Acts 4:24   Ephesians 4:11-15

Romans 4:17   Philippians 4:19

1 Corinthians 1:10   Romans 5:5

Acts 4:29   1 Corinthians 3:9

Mark 16:20b   Psalm 63:4

Exodus 35:35

This prayer was written by and used with the permission of T.R.
King; Valley Christian Center; Roanoke, Virginia.

Ministers

Father, in the name of Jesus, we pray and confess that the Spirit of the Lord shall rest upon _____: the spirit of wisdom and understanding, the spirit of counsel and might, the spirit of knowledge. We pray that as Your Spirit rests upon _____ He will make him/her of quick understanding because You, Lord, have anointed and qualified him/her to preach the Gospel to the meek, the poor, the wealthy, the afflicted. You have sent _____ to bind up and heal the brokenhearted, to proclaim liberty to the physical and spiritual captives and the opening of the prison and of the eyes to those who are bound.

_____ shall be called the priest of the Lord. People will speak of him/her as a minister of God. He/she shall eat the wealth of the nations.

We pray and believe that no weapon that is formed against _____ shall prosper and that any tongue that rises against him/her in judgment shall be shown to be in the wrong. We pray that You prosper _____ abundantly, Lord—physically, spiritually and financially.

We confess that _____ holds fast and follows the pattern of wholesome and sound teaching in all faith and love which is for us in Christ Jesus. _____ guards and keeps with the greatest love the precious and excellently adapted truth which has been entrusted to him/her by the Holy Spirit Who makes His home in _____.

Lord, we pray and believe that, each and every day, freedom and utterance is given _____, that he/she will open his/her mouth boldly and courageously as he/she ought to do to get the Gospel to the people. Thank You, Lord, for the added strength which comes superhumanly which You have given him/her.

We hereby confess that we shall stand behind _____ and undergird him/her in prayer. We will say only that good thing that will edify _____. We will not allow ourselves to judge him/her, but will continue to intercede for him/her and speak and pray blessings upon him/her in the name of Jesus. Thank You, Jesus, for the answers. Hallelujah! Amen.

Scripture References

Isaiah 11:2,3	2 Timothy 1:13,14 AMP
Isaiah 61:1,6 AMP	Ephesians 6:19,20 AMP
Isaiah 54:17 AMP	1 Peter 3:12

Missionaries

Father, we lift before You those in the Body of Christ who are out in the field carrying the good news of the Gospel—not only in this country but also around the world. We lift those in the Body of Christ who are suffering persecution—those who are in prison for their beliefs. Father, we know that You watch over Your Word to perform it, that Your Word prospers in the thing for which You sent it. Therefore, we speak Your Word and establish Your covenant on this earth. We pray here, and others receive the answer by the Holy Spirit.

Thank You, Father, for revealing unto Your people the integrity of Your Word and that they must be firm in faith against the devil's onset, withstanding him. Father, You are their Light, Salvation, Refuge and Stronghold. You hide them in Your shelter and set them high upon a rock. It is Your will that each one prospers, is in good health and lives in victory. You set the prisoners free, feed the hungry, execute justice, rescue and deliver.

We commission the ministering spirits to go forth and provide the necessary help for and assistance

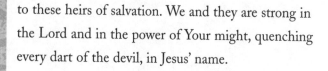
to these heirs of salvation. We and they are strong in the Lord and in the power of Your might, quenching every dart of the devil, in Jesus' name.

Father, we use our faith, covering these in the Body of Christ with Your Word. We say that no weapon formed against them shall prosper; and any tongue that rises against them in judgment, they shall show to be in the wrong. This peace, security and triumph over opposition is their inheritance as Your children. This is the righteousness which they obtain from You, Father, which You impart to them as their justification. They are far from even the thought of destruction; for they shall not fear, and terror shall not come near them.

Father, You say You will establish them to the end—keep them steadfast, give them strength and guarantee their vindication, that is, be their warrant against all accusation or indictment. They are not anxious beforehand how they shall reply in defense or what they are to say, for the Holy Spirit teaches them in that very hour and moment what they ought to say to those in the outside word, their speech being seasoned with salt.

We commit these our brothers and sisters in the Lord to You, Father, deposited into Your charge, entrusting them to Your protection and care, for You are faithful. You strengthen them and set them on a firm foundation and guard them from the evil one. We join our voices in praise unto You, Most High, that You might silence the enemy and avenger. Praise the Lord! Greater is He Who is in us than he who is in the world!

In Jesus' name we pray, amen.

Scripture References

Jeremiah 1:12	Ephesians 6:10,16
Isaiah 55:11	Isaiah 54:14,17
1 Peter 5:9	1 Corinthians 1:8
Psalm 27:1,5	Luke 12:11,12
3 John 2	Colossians 4:6
1 John 5:4,5	Acts 20:32
Psalm 146:7	2 Thessalonians 3:3
Psalm 144:7	Psalm 8:2
Matthew 18:18	1 John 4:4
Hebrews 1:14	

Revival

Father, in the name of Jesus, You have revived us again that Your people may rejoice in You. Thank You for showing us Your mercy and lovingkindness, O Lord, and for granting us Your salvation. You have created in us a clean heart, O God, and renewed a right, persevering and steadfast spirit within us. You have restored unto us the joy of Your salvation, and You are upholding us with a willing spirit. Now we will teach transgressors Your ways, and sinners shall be converted and return to You.

We therefore cleanse our ways by taking heed and keeping watch [on ourselves] according to Your Word [conforming our lives to it]. Since Your [great] promises are ours, we cleanse ourselves from everything that contaminates and defiles our bodies and spirits, and bring [our] consecration to completeness in the (reverential) fear of God. With our whole hearts have we sought You, inquiring for You and of You and yearning for You; O let us not wander or step aside [either in ignorance or willfully] from Your commandments. Your Word have we laid up in our hearts, that we might not sin against You.

Jesus, thank You for cleansing us through the Word—the teachings—which You have given us. We delight ourselves in Your statutes; we will not forget Your Word. Deal bountifully with Your servants, that we may live; and we will observe Your Word [hearing, receiving, loving and obeying it].

Father, in the name of Jesus, we are doers of the Word and not merely listeners to it. It is You, O Most High, Who have revived and stimulated us according to Your Word! Thank You for turning away our eyes from beholding vanity [idols and idolatry]; and restoring us to vigorous life and health in Your ways. Behold, we long for Your precepts; in Your righteousness give us renewed life. This is our comfort and consolation in our affliction: that Your Word has revived us and given us life.

We strip ourselves of our former natures—put off and discard our old, unrenewed selves—which characterized our previous manner of life. We are constantly renewed in the spirit of our minds—having a fresh mental and spiritual attitude; and we put on the new

nature (the regenerate self) created in God's image,
(Godlike) in true righteousness and holiness. Though
our outer man is (progressively) decaying and wasting
away, our inner self is being (progressively) renewed day
after day. Hallelujah! Amen.

Scripture References (AMP)

Psalm 85:6,7	James 1:22
Psalm 51:10,12,13	Psalm 119:25
Psalm 119:9-11	Psalm 119:37,40,50
2 Corinthians 7:1	Ephesians 4:22-24
John 15:3	2 Corinthians 4:16b
Psalm 119:16,17	

Success of a Conference

Father, Jesus said whatever we bind on earth is bound in heaven, and whatever we loose on earth is loosed in heaven. In His name we bind the will of each person, psalmist, speaker, usher, and worker to your will, their minds to the mind of Christ, and their emotions to the control of the Holy Spirit.

Let it be known and understood by all that it is in the name and through the power and authority of Jesus Christ of Nazareth and by means of Him that this conference is successful.

The speakers shall be filled with and controlled by the Holy Spirit. When the people see the boldness and unfettered eloquence of the speakers, they shall marvel and recognize that they have been with Jesus. Everybody shall be praising and glorifying God for what shall be occurring. By the hands of the ministers, numerous and startling signs and wonders will be performed among the people.

Father, in the name of Jesus, we thank You that You have observed the enemy's threats and have granted us,

Your bondservants, full freedom to declare Your message fearlessly—while You stretch out Your hand to cure and perform signs and wonders through the authority and by the power of the name of Your Holy Child and Servant, Jesus.

We thank You, Father, that when we pray, the place in which we are assembled will be shaken; and we shall all be filled with the Holy Spirit, and Your people shall continue to speak the Word of God with freedom and boldness and courage.

By common consent, we shall all meet together at the conference. More and more individuals shall join themselves with us—a crowd of both men and women. The people shall gather from the North, South, East and West, bringing the sick and those troubled with foul spirits, and they shall all be cured.

Thank You, Father, that our speakers are men and women of good and attested character and repute, full of the Holy Spirit and wisdom. The people who shall hear will not be able to resist the intelligence and the wisdom and the inspiration of the Spirit with which they speak, in the name of Jesus.

Thank You, Father, for the performance of Your Word in the name of Jesus! Amen.

Scripture References (AMP)

Acts 4:10,13,21

Acts 5:12a

Acts 4:29-31

Acts 5:12b,13,16

Acts 6:3,10

Protection and Deliverance of a City

Father, in the name of Jesus, we have received Your power—ability, efficiency and might—because the Holy Spirit has come upon us; and we are Your witnesses in _____ and to the ends—the very bounds—of the earth.

We fearlessly and confidently and boldly draw near to the throne of grace that we may receive mercy and find grace to help in good time for every need—appropriate help and well-timed help, coming just when we in the city of _____ need it.

Father, thank You for sending forth Your commandments to the earth; Your Word runs very swiftly throughout _____. Your Word continues to grow and spread.

Father, you see the regional and cultural strongholds that would hinder the Gospel. You have told us to declare your works. So we say boldly that the prince of the power of the air, the god of this world who blinds the unbelievers' minds (that they should not discern the truth) is a defeated foe. We declare on the authority of

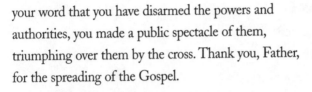

your word that you have disarmed the powers and authorities, you made a public spectacle of them, triumphing over them by the cross. Thank you, Father, for the spreading of the Gospel.

Holy Spirit, we ask You to visit our city and open the eyes of the people, that they may turn from darkness to light, and from the power of Satan to God, so that they may thus receive forgiveness and release from their sins and a place and portion among those who are consecrated and purified by faith in Jesus.

Father, we pray for deliverance and salvation for those who are following the course and fashion of this world—who are under the sway of the tendency of this present age—following the prince of the power of the air.

Father, forgive them, for they know not what they do.

Father, You see the regional and cultural strong-holds that would hinder the Gospel. You have told us to declare Your works. So we say boldly that the prince of the power of the air, the god of this world who blinds the unbelievers' minds (that they should not discern the truth) is a defeated foe. We declare on the authority of

Your Word that You have disarmed the powers and authorities, You made a public spectacle of them, triumphing over them by the cross. Thank You, Father, for the spreading of the Gospel.

Thank You, Father, for the guardian angels assigned to this place who war for us in the heavenlies.

In the name of Jesus, we stand victorious over the principalities, powers, rulers of the darkness of this world and spiritual wickedness in high places over _____.

We ask the Holy Spirit to sweep through the gates of our city and convince the people and bring demonstration to them about sin and about righteousness—uprightness of heart and right standing with God—and about judgment.

Father, You said, **For I know the thoughts and plans that I have for you . . . thoughts and plans for welfare and peace, and not for evil, to give you hope in your final outcome** (Jer. 29:11 AMP). By the blessing of the influence of the upright and God's favor [because of them] the city of _____ is exalted. Amen.

Scripture References

Acts 1:8 AMP

Hebrews 4:16 AMP

Psalm 147:15 AMP

Acts 12:24 AMP

Jeremiah 29:7,8

Psalm 55:9 AMP

Acts 26:18

Ephesians 2:2 AMP

Luke 23:34a AMP

2 Corinthians 4:4 AMP

Ephesians 6:12

Psalm 101:8 AMP

John 16:8 AMP

Jeremiah 29:11 AMP

Proverbs 11:11a AMP

School Systems and Children

Father, we thank You that the entrance of Your Word brings light and that You watch over Your Word to perform it. Father, we bring before You the _____ school system(s) and the men and women who are in positions of authority within the school system(s).

We ask You to give them skillful and godly wisdom, that Your knowledge might be pleasant to them. Then discretion will watch over them; understanding will keep them and deliver them from the way of evil and from evil men. We pray that men and women of integrity, blameless and complete in Your sight, remain in these positions, but that the wicked be cut off and the treacherous be rooted out in the name of Jesus. Father, we thank You for born-again, Spirit-filled people in these positions.

Father, we bring our children, our young people, before You. We speak forth Your Word boldly and confidently, Father, that we and our households are saved in the name of Jesus. We are redeemed from the curse of the law, for Jesus was made a curse for us. *Our sons and daughters are not given to another people.* We enjoy our children, and they shall not go into captivity, in the name of Jesus.

As parents, we train our children in the way they should go, and when they are old they shall not depart from it.

Our children shrink from whatever might offend You, Father, and discredit the name of Christ. They show themselves to be blameless, guileless, innocent, and uncontaminated children of God, without blemish (faultless, unrebukable), in the midst of a crooked and wicked generation, holding out to it and offering to all the Word of Life. Thank You, Father, that You give them knowledge and skill in all learning and wisdom and bring them into favor with those around them.

Father, we pray and intercede that these young people, their parents, and the leaders in the school system(s) separate themselves from contact with contaminating and corrupting influences and cleanse themselves from everything that would contaminate and defile their spirits, souls, and bodies. We confess that they shun immorality and all sexual looseness — flee from impurity in thought, word, or deed — and they live and conduct themselves honorably and becomingly as in the open light of day. We confess and believe that they shun youthful lusts and flee from them in the name of Jesus.

Father, we ask You to commission the ministering spirits to go forth and police the area, dispelling the forces of darkness.

Father, we thank You that in Christ all the treasures of divine wisdom (of comprehensive insight into the ways and purposes of God) and all the riches of spiritual knowledge and enlightenment are stored up and lie hidden for us, and we walk in Him.

We praise You, Father, that we shall see _____ walking in the ways of piety and virtue, revering Your name, Father. Those who err in spirit will come to understanding, and those who murmur discontentedly will accept instruction in the way, Jesus, to Your will and carry out Your purposes in their lives; for You, Father, occupy first place in their hearts. We surround _____ with our faith.

Thank You, Father, that You are the delivering God. Thank You that the good news of the Gospel is published throughout our school system(s). Thank You for intercessors to stand on Your Word and for laborers of the harvest to preach Your Word in Jesus' name. Praise the Lord! Amen.

Scripture References

Psalm 119:130	2 Timothy 2:21 AMP
Jeremiah 1:12	2 Corinthians 7:1 AMP
Proverbs 2:10-12 AMP	1 Corinthians 6:18 AMP
Proverbs 2:21,22 AMP	Romans 13:13 AMP
Acts 16:31	Ephesians 5:4
Galatians 3:13	2 Timothy 2:22
Deuteronomy 28:32,41	Matthew 18:18
Proverbs 22:6 AMP	2 Timothy 2:26
Philippians 2:15,16 AMP	Hebrews 1:14
Daniel 1:17 AMP	Colossians 2:3 AMP
Daniel 1:9	Isaiah 29:23,24 AMP
1 John 2:16,17 AMP	

American Government

Father, in Jesus' name, we give thanks for the
United States and its government. We hold up in prayer
before You the men and women who are in positions of
authority. We pray and intercede for the president, the
representatives, the senators, the judges of our land, the
policemen and the policewomen, as well as the gover-
nors and mayors and for all those who are in authority
over us in any way. We pray that the Spirit of the Lord
rests upon them.

We believe that skillful and godly wisdom has
entered into the heart of our president and knowledge is
pleasant to him. Discretion watches over him; understanding keeps him and delivers him from the way of
evil and from evil men.

Father, we ask that You compass the president
about with men and women who make their hearts and
ears attentive to godly counsel and do that which is
right in Your sight. We believe You cause them to be
men and women of integrity who are obedient concerning us that we may lead a quiet and peaceable life in all

godliness and honesty. We pray that the upright shall dwell in our government, that men and women blameless and complete in Your sight, Father, shall remain in these positions of authority; but the wicked shall be cut off from our government and the treacherous shall be rooted out of it.

Your Word declares that **blessed is the nation whose God is the Lord** (Ps. 33:12). We receive Your blessing. Father, You are our Refuge and Stronghold in times of trouble (high cost, destitution and desperation). So we declare with our mouths that Your people dwell safely in this land, and we *prosper* abundantly. We are more than conquerors through Christ Jesus!

It is written in Your Word that the heart of the king is in the hand of the Lord, and you turn it whichever way You desire. We believe the heart of our leader is in Your hand and that his decisions are directed of the Lord.

We give thanks unto You that the good news of the Gospel is published in our land. The Word of the Lord prevails and grows mightily in the hearts and lives of the people. We give thanks for this land and the leaders You have given to us, in Jesus' name.

Jesus is Lord over the United States! Amen.

Scripture References

1 Timothy 2:1-3   Deuteronomy 28:10,11

Proverbs 2:10-12,21,22   Romans 8:37 AMP

Psalm 33:12   Proverbs 21:1

Psalm 9:9   Acts 12:24

Members of the Armed Forces

Father, our troops have been sent into
_____ as peacekeepers. We petition You,
Lord, according to Psalm 91, for the safety of our military personnel.

This is no afternoon athletic contest that our armed forces will walk away from and forget about in a couple of hours. This is for keeps, a life-or-death fight to the finish against the devil and all his angels. We look beyond human instruments of conflict and address the forces and authorities and rulers of darkness and powers in the spiritual world. As children of the Most High God we enforce the triumphant victory of our Lord Jesus Christ.

Our Lord stripped principalities and powers, making a show of them openly. Thank You, Jesus, for defeating the evil one and his forces of darkness for us, and giving us authority to proclaim Your name that is above every name. All power and authority both in heaven and earth belong to You. Righteousness and

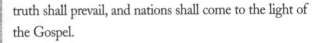
truth shall prevail, and nations shall come to the light of the Gospel.

We petition heaven to turn our troops into a real peacekeeping force by pouring out the glory of God through our men and women in that part of the world. Use them as instruments of righteousness to defeat the plans of the devil.

Lord, we plead the power of the blood of Jesus, asking You to manifest Your power and glory. We entreat You on behalf of the citizens in these countries on both sides of this conflict. They have experienced pain and heartache; they are victims of the devil's strategies to steal, kill and destroy. We pray that they will come to know Jesus Who came to give us life, and life more abundantly.

We stand in the gap for the people of the war-torn, devil-overrun land. We expect an overflowing of Your goodness and glory in the lives of those for whom we are praying. May they call upon Your name and be saved.

You, Lord, make known Your salvation; Your righteousness You openly show in the sight of the nations.

Father, provide for and protect the families of our armed forces. Preserve marriages, cause the hearts of

the parents to turn toward their children and the hearts
of the children to turn toward the fathers and mother.
We plead the blood of Jesus over our troops and their
families. Provide a support system to undergird, uplift
and edify those who have been left to raise children by
themselves. Jesus has been made unto these parents
wisdom, righteousness and sanctification. Through
Your Holy Spirit, comfort the lonely and strengthen
the weary.

Father, we are looking forward to that day when
the whole earth shall be filled with the knowledge of the
Lord as the waters cover the sea.

In Jesus' name, amen.

Scripture References

Ephesians 6:12 MESSAGE   Psalm 98:2 AMP

Colossians 2:15   Malachi 4:6

John 10:10   1 Corinthians 1:30

Ezekiel 22:30   Isaiah 11:9

Acts 2:21

A portion of this prayer was taken from a letter dated January
22, 1996, written by Kenneth Copeland of Kenneth Copeland
Ministries in Fort Worth, Texas, and sent to his partners. Used
by permission.

The Nation and People of Israel

Lord, You will not cast off nor spurn Your people; neither will You abandon Your heritage. You have regard for the covenant [You made with Abraham]. Father, remember Your covenant with Abraham, Isaac and Jacob.

Father, we pray for the peace of Jerusalem. May they prosper who love you [the Holy City]. May peace be within your walls and prosperity within your palaces! For our brethren and companions' sake, we will now say, "Peace be within you! For the sake of the house of the Lord our God, we will seek, inquire for and require your good."

Father, we thank You for bringing the people of Israel into unity with each other and for bringing Your Church (both Jew and Gentile) into oneness—one new man. Thank You for the peace treaties with Israel's former enemies. May these treaties be used for good to make way for the good news of the Gospel as we prepare for the coming of our Messiah.

We intercede for those who have become callously indifferent (blinded, hardened and made insensible to the Gospel). We pray that they will not fall to their utter spiritual ruin. It was through their false step and transgression that salvation has come to the Gentiles. Now, we ask that the eyes of their understanding be enlightened that they may know the Messiah Who will make Himself known to all of Israel.

We ask You to strengthen the house of Judah and save the house of Joseph. Thank You, Father, for restoring them because You have compassion on them. We thank You for Your great mercy and love to them and to us, in the name of Yeshua, our Messiah.

Father, thank You for saving Israel and gathering them from the nations, that they may give thanks to Your holy name and glory in Your praise. Praise be to You, Lord, the God of Israel, from everlasting to everlasting. Let all the people say, "Amen!" Praise the Lord.

In Jesus' name, amen.

Scripture References

Psalm 94:14   Romans 11:7

Psalm 74:20 AMP

Leviticus 46:22

Psalm 122:6-9 AMP

Ephesians 1:18

Romans 11:11 AMP

Ephesians 2:14 AMP

Zechariah 10:6,12 NIV

Psalm 106:47,48 NIV

Praying the Scriptures

> ...The earnest (heart-felt, continued)
> prayer of a righteous man makes tremendous
> power available—dynamic in its working.

> **James 5:16** AMP

Prayer is fellowshiping with the Father—a vital, personal contact with God Who is more than enough. We are to be in constant communion with Him:

> For the eyes of the Lord are upon the
> righteous—those who are upright and in right
> standing with God—and His ears are attentive
> (open) to their prayer....

> **1 Peter 3:12** AMP

Prayer is not to be a religious form with no power. It is to be effective and accurate and bring *results*. God watches over His Word to perform it (Jer. 1:12).

Prayer that brings results must be based on God's Word.

For the Word that God speaks is alive and
full of power—making it active, operative,
energizing and effective; it is sharper than any
two-edged sword, penetrating to the dividing
line of the breath of life (soul) and [the immor-
tal] spirit, and of joints and marrow [that is, of
the deepest parts of our nature] exposing and
sifting and analyzing and judging the very
thoughts and purposes of the heart.

Hebrews 4:12 AMP

Prayer is this "living" Word in our mouths. Our
mouths must speak forth faith, for faith is what pleases
God (Heb. 11:6). We hold His Word up to Him in
prayer, and our Father sees Himself in His Word.

God's Word is our contact with Him. We put Him
in remembrance of His Word (Isa. 43:26) placing a
demand on His ability, in the name of our Lord Jesus.
We remind Him that He supplies all of our needs
according to His riches in glory by Christ Jesus (Phil.
4:19). That Word does not return to Him void—
without producing any effect, useless—but it *shall*
accomplish that which He pleases and purposes, and it

shall prosper in the thing for which He sent it (Isa. 55:11). Hallelujah!

God did *not* leave us without His thoughts and His ways, for we have His Word—His bond. God instructs us to call Him, and He will answer and show us great and mighty things (Jer. 33:3). Prayer is to be exciting—not drudgery.

It takes someone to pray. God moves as we pray in faith—believing. He says that His eyes run to and fro throughout the whole earth to show Himself strong on behalf of those whose hearts are blameless toward Him. (2 Chron. 16:9). We are blameless (Eph. 1:4). We are His very own children (Eph. 1:5). We are His righteousness in Christ Jesus (2 Cor. 5:21). He tells us to come boldly to the throne of grace and *obtain* mercy and find grace to help in time of need—appropriate and well-timed help (Heb. 4:16). Praise the Lord!

The prayer armor is for every believer, every member of the Body of Christ who will put it on and walk in it, for the weapons of our warfare are *not carnal* but mighty through God for the pulling down of the strongholds of the enemy (Satan, the god of this world, and all his demonic forces). Spiritual warfare takes place in prayer (2 Cor. 10:4, Eph. 6:12,18).

There are many different kinds of prayer, such as the prayer of thanksgiving and praise, the prayer of dedication and worship and the prayer that changes *things* (not God). All prayer involves a time of fellow-shiping with the Father.

In Ephesians 6, we are instructed to take the Sword of the Spirit, which is the Word of God, and **pray at all times—on every occasion, in every season—in the Spirit, with all [manner of] prayer and entreaty** (Eph. 6:18 AMP).

In 1 Timothy 2 we are admonished and urged that **petitions, prayers, intercessions and thanksgivings be offered on behalf of all men** (1 Tim. 2:1 AMP). *Prayer is our responsibility.*

Prayer must be the foundation of every Christian endeavor. Any failure is a prayer failure. We are *not* to be ignorant concerning God's Word. God desires for His people to be successful, to be filled with a full, deep and clear knowledge of His will (His Word) and to bear fruit in every good work (Col. 1:9-13). We then bring honor and glory to Him (John 15:8). He desires that we know how to pray, for **the prayer of the upright is his delight** (Prov. 15:8).

Our Father has not left us helpless. Not only has He given us His Word, but also He has given us the Holy Spirit to help our infirmities when we know not how to pray as we ought (Rom. 8:26). Praise God! Our Father has provided His people with every possible avenue to ensure their complete and total victory in this life in the name of our Lord Jesus (1 John 5:3-5).

We pray to the Father, in the name of Jesus, through the Holy Spirit, according to the Word!

Using God's Word on purpose, specifically, in prayer is one means of prayer, and it is a most effective and accurate means. Jesus said, **The words (truths) that I have been speaking to you are spirit and life** (John 6:63 AMP).

When Jesus faced Satan in the wilderness, He said, "It is written...it is written...it is written." We are to live, be upheld and sustained by every Word that proceeds from the mouth of God (Matt. 4:4).

James, by the Spirit, admonishes that we do not have because we do not ask. We ask and receive not, because we ask amiss (James 4:2,3). We must heed that admonishment now, for we are to become experts in prayer, rightly dividing the Word of Truth (2 Tim. 2:15).

Using the Word in prayer is *not* taking it out of context, for His Word in us is the key to answered prayer—to prayer that brings results. He is able to do exceeding abundantly above all we ask or think, according to the power that works in us (Eph. 3:20). The power lies within God's Word. It is anointed by the Holy Spirit. The Spirit of God does not lead us apart from the Word, for the Word is of the Spirit of God. We apply that Word personally to ourselves and to others—not adding to or taking from it—in the name of Jesus. We apply the Word to the *now*—to those things, circumstances and situations facing each of us *now*.

Paul was very specific and definite in his praying. The first chapters of Ephesians, Philippians, Colossians and 2 Thessalonians are examples of how Paul prayed for believers. There are numerous others. *Search them out.* Paul wrote under the inspiration of the Holy Spirit. We can use these Spirit-given prayers today!

In 2 Corinthians 1:11, 2 Corinthians 9:14 and
Philippians 1:4, we see examples of how believers prayed
one for another—putting others first in their prayer life
with *joy*. Our faith does work by love (Gal. 5:6). We
grow spiritually as we reach out to help others—praying
for and with them and holding out to them the Word
of Life (Phil. 2:16).

Man is a spirit, he has a soul and he lives in a body
(1 Thess. 5:23). In order to operate successfully, each of
these three parts must be fed properly. The soul, or
intellect, feeds on intellectual food to produce intellectual strength. The body feeds on physical food to
produce physical strength. The spirit—the heart or
inward man—is the real you, the part that has been
reborn in Christ Jesus. It must feed on spirit food,
which is God's Word, in order to produce and develop
faith. As we feast upon God's Word, our minds become
renewed with His Word, and we have a fresh mental
and spiritual attitude (Eph. 4:23,24).

Likewise, we are to present our bodies a living
sacrifice, holy, acceptable unto God (Rom. 12:1) and not
let that body dominate us, but bring it into subjection to
the spirit man (1 Cor. 9:27). God's Word is healing and

health to all our flesh (Prov. 4:22). Therefore, God's Word affects each part of us—spirit, soul and body. We become vitally united to the Father, to Jesus and to the Holy Spirit—one with Them. (John 16:13-15, John 17:21, Col. 2:10.)

God's Word, this spirit food, takes root in our hearts, is formed by the tongue and is spoken out of our mouths. This is creative power. The spoken Word works as we confess it and then apply the action to it.

Be doers of the Word, and not hearers only, deceiving your own selves (James 1:22). Faith without works, or corresponding action, is *dead* (James 2:17). Don't be mental assenters—those who agree that the Bible is true but never act on it. *Real faith is acting on God's Word now.* We cannot build faith without practicing the Word. We cannot develop an effective prayer life that is anything but empty words unless God's Word actually has a part in our lives. We are to hold fast to our *confession* of the Word's truthfulness. Our Lord Jesus is the High Priest of our confession (Heb. 3:1), and He is the Guarantee of a better agreement—a more excellent and advantageous covenant (Heb. 7:22).

Prayer does not cause faith to work, but faith causes prayer to work. Therefore, any prayer problem is a problem of doubt—doubting the integrity of the Word and the ability of God to stand behind His promises or the statements of fact in the Word.

We can spend fruitless hours in prayer if our hearts are not prepared beforehand. Preparation of the heart, the spirit, comes from meditation in the Father's Word, meditation on who we are in Christ, what He is to us and what the Holy Spirit can mean to us as we become God-inside minded. As God told Joshua (Josh. 1:8), as we meditate on the Word day and night, and do according to all that is written, then shall we make our way prosperous and have good success. We are to attend to God's Word, submit to His sayings, keep them in the center of our hearts and put away contrary talk (Prov. 4:20-24).

When we use God's Word in prayer, this is *not* something we just rush through uttering once and we are finished. Do *not* be mistaken. There is nothing "magical" nor "manipulative" about it—no set pattern or device in order to satisfy what we want or think out of our flesh. Instead we are holding God's Word before Him. We confess what He says belongs to us.

We expect His divine intervention while we choose not to look at the things that are seen but at the things that are unseen, for the things that are seen are subject to change (2 Cor. 4:18).

Prayer based upon the Word rises above the senses, contacts the Author of the Word and sets His spiritual laws into motion. It is not just saying prayers that get results, but it is spending time with the Father, learning His wisdom, drawing on His strength, being filled with His quietness and basking in His love that brings results to our prayers. Praise the Lord!

The prayers in this book are designed to teach and train you in the art of personal confession and intercessory prayer. As you pray them, you will be reinforcing the prayer armor which we have been instructed to put on in Ephesians 6:11. The fabric from which the armor is made is the Word of God. We are to live by every word that proceeds from the mouth of God. We desire the whole counsel of God, because we know it changes us. By receiving that counsel, you will be **...transformed (changed) by the [entire] renewal of your mind—by its new ideals and attitude—so that you may prove [for yourselves] what is the good and acceptable and perfect will of God, even the thing which is good and acceptable and perfect [in His sight for you]** (Rom. 12:2 AMP).

The prayers of personal confession of the Word of God for yourself can also be used as intercessory prayers for others by simply praying them in the third person, changing the pronouns *I* or *we* to the name(s) of the person or persons for whom you are interceding and adjusting the verbs accordingly.

The prayers of intercession have blanks in which you (individually or as a group) are to fill in the spaces with the name(s) of the person(s) for whom you are praying. These prayers of intercession can likewise be made into prayers of personal confession for yourself (or your group) by inserting your own name(s) and the proper personal pronouns in the appropriate places.

An often-asked question is this: "How many times should I pray the same prayer?"

The answer is simple: You pray until you know that the answer is fixed in your heart. After that, you need to repeat the prayer whenever adverse circumstances or long delays cause you to be tempted to doubt that your prayer has been heard and your request granted.

The Word of God is your weapon against the temptation to lose heart and grow weary in your prayer life. When that Word of promise becomes fixed in your heart, you will find yourself praising, giving glory to God for the answer, even when the only evidence you have of that answer is your own faith.

Another question often asked is this: "When we repeat prayers more than once, aren't we praying 'vain repetitions'?"

Obviously, such people are referring to the admonition of Jesus when He told His disciples: **And when you pray do not (multiply words, repeating the same ones over and over, and) heap up phrases as the Gentiles do, for they think they will be heard for their much speaking** (Matt. 6:7 AMP). Praying the Word of God is not praying the kind of prayer that the "heathen" pray. You will note in 1 Kings 18:25-29 the manner of prayer that was offered to the gods who could not hear. That is not the way you and I pray. The words that we speak are not in vain, but they are spirit and life and mighty through God to the pulling down of strongholds. We have a God Whose eyes are over the righteous and Whose ears are open to us: When we pray, He hears us.

You are the righteousness of God in Christ Jesus, and your prayers will avail much. They will bring salvation to the sinner, deliverance to the oppressed, healing to the sick and prosperity to the poor. They will usher in the next move of God in the earth. In addition to affecting outward circumstances and other people, your prayers will also have an effect on you.

In the very process of praying, your life will be changed as you go from faith to faith and from glory to glory.

As a Christian, your first priority is to love the Lord your God with your entire being, and your neighbor as yourself. You are called to be an intercessor, a man or woman of prayer. You are to seek the face of the Lord as you inquire, listen, meditate and consider in the temple of the Lord.

As one of "God's set-apart ones," the will of the
Lord for your life is the same as it is for the life of every
other true believer: ...**seek ye first the kingdom of God,
and his righteousness; and all these things shall be
added unto you** (Matt. 6:33).

About the Author

Germaine Griffin Copeland, founder and president of Word Ministries, Inc., is the author of the *Prayers That Avail Much* family of books. Her writings provide scriptural prayer instruction to help you pray effectively for those things that concern you and your family and for other prayer assignments. Her teachings on prayer, the personal growth of the intercessor, emotional healing, and related subjects have brought understanding, hope, healing, and liberty to the discouraged and emotionally wounded. She is a woman of prayer and praise whose highest form of worship is the study of God's Word. Her greatest desire is to know God.

Word Ministries, Inc. is a prayer and teaching ministry. Germaine believes that God has called her to teach the practical application of the Word of Truth for successful, victorious living. After years of searching diligently for truth and trying again and again to come out of depression, she decided that she was a mistake. Out of the depths of despair she called upon the name of the Lord, and the light of God's presence invaded the room where she was sitting.

It was in that moment that she experienced the warmth of God's love; old things passed away and she felt brand new. She discovered a motivation for living — life had purpose. Living in the presence of God she has found unconditional love and acceptance, healing for crippled emotions, contentment that overcomes depression, peace in the midst of adverse circumstances, and grace for developing healthy relationships. The ongoing process of transformation evolved into praying for others, and the prayer of intercession became her prayer focus.

Germaine is the daughter of Reverend A. H. "Buck" Griffin and the late Donnis Brock Griffin. She and her husband, Everette, have four children and their prayer assignments increase as grandchildren and great-grandchildren are born into the family. Germaine and Everette reside in Sandy Springs, a suburb of Atlanta, Georgia.

Word Ministries' offices are located in historic Roswell, 38 Sloan Street, Roswell, Georgia 30075. Telephone: 770-518-1065.

You may contact

Word Ministries

by writing

Word Ministries, Inc.

38 Sloan Street

Roswell, Georgia 30075

or by calling 770-518-1065

www.prayers.org

*Please include your testimonies
and praise reports when you write.*

MISSION STATEMENT
Word Ministries, Inc.

To motivate individuals to spiritual growth

and emotional wholeness,

encouraging them to become more deeply

and intimately acquainted

with the Father God

as they pray prayers that avail much.

OTHER BOOKS BY GERMAINE COPELAND

A Call to Prayer

The Road God Walks

Prayers That Avail Much Commemorative Gift Edition

Prayers That Avail Much Commemorative Leather Edition

Prayers That Avail Much for Business

Prayers That Avail Much Volume 1

Prayers That Avail Much Volume 1 — mass market edition

Prayers That Avail Much Volume 2

Prayers That Avail Much Volume 2 — mass market edition

Prayers That Avail Much Volume 3

Prayers That Avail Much Volume 3 — mass market edition

Prayers That Avail Much for Men

Prayers That Avail Much for Women

Prayers That Avail Much for Mothers — hardbound

Prayers That Avail Much for Mothers — paperback

Prayers That Avail Much for Teens

Prayers That Avail Much for Kids

Prayers That Avail Much for Kids — Book 2

Prayers That Avail Much for the Workplace

Oraciones Con Poder — *Prayers That Avail Much* (Spanish Edition)

Additional copies of this book are
available from your local bookstore.

Harrison House
Tulsa, Oklahoma 74153

THE HARRISON HOUSE VISION

Proclaiming the truth and the power

Of the Gospel of Jesus Christ

With excellence;

Challenging Christians to

Live victoriously,

Grow spiritually,

Know God intimately.